Silent Grief

by

Clara Hinton

New Leaf Press

First printing: February 1998

ISBN: 0-89221-371-X
Library of Congress Number: 97-75892

Cover by Left Coast Design, Portland, OR.

Printed in the United States of America.

Dedication:

For every parent who has entered
through the gates of child loss.

Acknowledgments

My heartfelt thanks to the many doctors, nurses, ministers, and other caring professionals who have helped me put this book into a practical perspective. A most special thanks to each and every parent who has allowed me to enter into that very private corner of the heart where so many tears have been shed. A very grateful thanks to my editor, Jim Fletcher, for working with me from beginning to end. And most of all thank you to my family for continually encouraging me to see this book through to completion.

A very special thanks to Mandy for her unending patience working with me at the computer.

Above all else, I thank God for granting me this most blessed privilege of sharing the thoughts contained in this book with you.

Contents

Introduction

Life is an exciting adventure. At least that's how we view life on most days. But sometimes adventures can lead us into treacherous waters, and we find ourselves holding our breath, clinging for dear life onto anything we can find. We desperately hope and pray that we will make it to a safe shore where we will find peace and rest.

When a parent is thrust into the deep sea of grief caused by losing a precious child, the waters are icy cold and the way seems so dark for such a long, lonely time. Calls for help often go unnoticed and the echoes are only those of silence. Fear, loneliness, and despair embrace our once-happy hearts, and our own tears fill the turbulent seas in which we are now forced to swim. As we struggle through this unknown path we often feel there is no way out. Our heavy hearts weigh us down and our grief puts a paralyzing grip on both body and soul.

If you are struggling to stay afloat in your grief, hold on tight. If your heart feels so heavy that you cannot seem to move, sit still. If your eyes hurt from shedding so many tears, gently close them and take a much-needed rest. There is help. There is hope. There is a way out of that swirling sea of grief. The seas will be rough at times. The journey may seem awfully lonely. But, the final destination will give you a peace beyond all human understanding.

If your heart has been broken by losing a child — your child — then the words in this book are for you. It is my most sincere prayer that you will find comfort for your hurting heart and the strength to move forward in life's journey. I pray that through this book you will find the full assurance that you have never really been alone. You have a Friend who is constant and true. Your silent grief has been heard by someone who sincerely cares.

May your heart be warmed and may your tears be gently dried. May you hold fast to the blessing of life and may love dwell within your soul forevermore.

Lovingly,
Clara Hinton

Part 1 — In the Valley

Chapter 1

I'm Sorry

I am weary with my sighing; every night I make
my bed swim, I dissolve my couch with tears. My eye
has wasted away with grief (Ps. 6:6-7).

"I'm sorry." Two very small, very used words. But, oh, the meaning those words can hold! Those two words, "I'm sorry," can change the course of a person's life forever, especially when connected to the loss of a child. Your child.

"I'm sorry" can come very early, even before the actual birth of a child, in the form of a miscarriage. Those words can ring in the ears of parents at birth when the beautiful baby they expected to take home with them has no life. Stillborn. "I'm sorry." Those words can echo in a parent's heart when a healthy child so full of beauty and life, takes a nap, never to wake again. The stealthy robber of young life, Sudden Infant Death Syndrome, takes your baby. "I'm sorry" can come later in life when a child has a totally unexpected accident, an accidental poison overdose, a fall into the swimming pool, or a disease that so fiercely attacks and just refuses to let go. "I'm sorry." Two words we very rarely like to hear. Two words we never want to hear when they are about our child.

Sometimes the bearer of the news is gentle; sometimes very abrupt. It really doesn't matter. The heart is still pierced and left with a gaping hole. A hole that hurts like nothing else in this world. There is no easy way to hear those words or gentle way to live with them. Not now, anyway.

In talking with many, many parents, I have found that the hardships of life itself can be brutally cruel. The stories that have been shared from each one who has suffered child loss have been heart-wrenching. Just hearing the words that a child has died brings most of us to our knees in tears. Children are not supposed to die. Especially not now. Not our children.

My own heart has been torn at several different times, and each time I heard those words, "I'm sorry," I wanted to run away. Scream. Hit something. Do anything to make the hurt go away. I wanted to go to bed for a long, long time and wake up to find out that it was only a bad dream. But, the bad dreams never go away. Never totally.

One of the saddest stories told to me was from a young lady that I didn't even know. She was working as a sales clerk at a store, watching me try to school shop with three of my very excited little ones. She began making small talk about how patient I was with the children. They seemed to be all over that store, and into just about everything. After exchanging the usual talk about school shopping, I asked the question, "Do you have any children?" "Yes," she said. And then the tears began to flow. She gave birth to a beautiful, perfect son 12 years ago, and all of life was wonderful. She bathed him one evening, rocked him to sleep as usual, and he slept through his night feeding. She awoke from habit, and peeped into the nursery. All looked well, so she enjoyed an extra hour of sleep. When he still had not woke up by 7:00 a.m. she decided to wake him. After all, he needed to be fed, and she wanted to hold him. He was adorable! As she touched him, she knew immediately. There would be no pulling him to her breast for a morning feeding. His little body was cold and so, so still. No movement. No waking. Only the silence that comes with death.

The next thing she remembers is her husband standing by her side as the paramedics placed her little son in a black bag and zipped it shut. She said that she wanted to scream, but nothing came out. Only bitter, bitter tears would fall.

The worst was not over, though. Because her son had died at home, the parents had to be questioned about their baby's death. She said the questions were at times accusatory in nature and harsh in content. After an hour of painful questioning, it was concluded that her beautiful son had died in his sleep of Sudden Infant Death Syndrome at the age of six months. He was gone. Forever. And "I'm sorry" was the best that the hospital staff could do. It was all that anyone did.

This young lady went on to tell a bittersweet story. It was a long journey from her tears to this day of talking to me, from her days of not wanting to get up and move, to getting a job and trying to live again. She and her husband had always wanted a large family. After five difficult, trying years she got pregnant again, and she delivered a two and one-half pound baby girl prematurely. Even though the little girl was a fighter, it was almost one entire year before she was ready to be released from the hospital. Instead of being a wonderful, peaceful, joyous time, it was a year of deep anxiety, never knowing from day to day if this little girl would live or die. There was a separation from her baby. And fear. That awful, crippling fear. A constant fear that none of her friends or family seemed to understand. A fear that she would lose this baby, too.

Twelve years later, she and her husband have their little girl, and no other children. She explained that for some unknown reason she cannot get pregnant again. She has had all of the fertility testing done. She's had genetic counseling. But nothing. No other children. The questions still come, though. She explained that her family and friends still tease her constantly about having another child. She said she wants to scream, "Don't you understand? I can't. I just can't!" Being unable to conceive again only adds to her grief. Shattered dream after dream. A heart that has been broken in two.

I asked if she got any help or ever attended any grief support meetings, and she quietly said she had not. She said, "At first I just couldn't be around other people. All I did was cry. Everyone kept saying to just have another baby, and I would feel better. That would take the hurt away. But, of course, I know that another baby doesn't take the hurt away. What helped? My faith. My prayers seemed to be the only thing that got me through.

"But, there's my husband. Our son's death is a closed issue with him. He refuses to talk about it. So I try to smile and be happy, but inside I feel so alone, and it still hurts so, so much. Thank you for listening."

This conversation took place over a year ago now, and it still haunts me. This young family suffered a severe blow to the heart, and there just didn't seem to be the kind of help available to them that they needed. The pain is still there, still hurting, still throbbing every day. But the grief is so silent now. No one seems to even understand. So why should they continue to bare their feelings and their souls to people, only to be hurt time and time again by people who do not feel what they feel? They simply find it easier not to talk.

Why did this young lady share her deep feelings with me, a total stranger? I wondered about that for a long, long time. The answer was in her closing words: "Thank you for listening." I did not have anything new to tell her that she had not already heard hundreds of times before. But I did listen. Hold on to that thought because it will be most important throughout the rest of this book. It is so very important to have someone who will listen. And to listen without passing judgment. God listens, and allows our tears to fall. He tenderly pays attention to each tear, and allows us time to really hear those words, "I'm sorry." This young lady and her husband need listeners, even 12 years after the death of their little boy. God listens. Why can't we?

Many may be wondering at this point why very early child loss is even brought up in this book. After all, in cases such as miscarriage parents haven't even seen their child, or named their child. We can somehow understand slightly the brief passing of pain with the SIDS baby, but miscarriage . . . that's another story. Most times, when child loss occurs very early in pregnancy, the gender of the child is not known. Many physicians will use the term "fetal tissue." A woman will say, however, "baby." Many may ask what the big upset is with losing a baby that you have never seen, held, or heard. The woman's body will be back to functioning normally again in six to eight weeks, and she can try to have another child if she so desires. Besides that, the rate of miscarriage is at least 20 percent of all pregnancies, and possibly higher. To many people, miscarriage is just a percentage — a number. Ask the mother and father who have suffered a miscarriage, and they may tell you something quite different. They experience a very painful loss. A grievous loss. And so few people can even begin to understand.

It is probably extremely difficult to understand a couple's

grief over early child loss unless you have personally been there, or know someone close to you who has been there. While the number of miscarriages are high, very few people will talk about them. Why? Child loss at any stage is a difficult topic to discuss, even between the couples who have themselves suffered the loss. Also, most people are made to feel uncomfortable around someone who cries, or who says that they are grieving. We would much rather talk about the weather than the loss of a child. The weather changes from day-to-day; child loss is here forever. And, there is the age-old belief that one should be able to quickly brush one's self off, pick up the pieces, and get on with life. In the case of miscarriage, the underlying belief seems to be that if you just have another baby immediately all will be well. I really wish that this misconception could be straightened out. You can never replace babies or children of any age. Yes, having another baby can bring joy to your life, but in no way does that child ever, ever replace your loss. Never. And for those couples who can no longer conceive, this idea of having another child is devastating to their grief.

My first miscarriage was a total nightmare, and has had a bearing on my entire life. My first pregnancy was a breeze. I delivered a perfect 8 pound, 8 ounce baby girl. I barely experienced morning sickness, and I only gained 20 pounds during pregnancy. My husband and I were as proud and happy as any couple could be. We always wanted a large family, so a year after Michelle was born, we decided to have another baby. I got pregnant immediately, had my first prenatal visit, and life was wonderful — until January 8. I noticed a tiny bit of a blood stain in my underwear. I looked in my little pregnancy book that the doctor had given me, and there was one very brief paragraph titled "Miscarriage." To tell you the honest truth, I did not even know what a miscarriage was. All that was said in the book was that some pregnancies end early. If you experience any bleeding, contact your doctor. I didn't consider a speck of blood to mean bleeding, so I went on through the day as usual.

Towards evening, however, I now had red blood, but not much. We were in the process of moving, so I thought that maybe I lifted something too heavy which caused slight bleeding from a strain. I briefly mentioned seeing some blood to my husband before going to bed. Neither one of us got upset. After all, the book said to call the doctor if bleeding occurred. This was only a few spots of blood. By morning, the bed was soaked in blood, and I felt weak. I had a sick feeling now that something was very, very wrong.

I remember so vividly that it was a beautiful, sunny Oklahoma City morning. But, our day felt darker than dark. My husband had the doctor paged. He was in church, and waited two hours to return our call. He said, very matter-of-factly, "You may be losing the baby. You will probably have several hours of severe bleeding and passing of tissue. Look for gray matter. That will indicate pregnancy loss."

We couldn't believe this was happening! We didn't even understand completely what was happening. Answers were vague. Information was not available. We called a friend, an older lady we knew from church, to come be with us. We were over a thousand miles away from home and had no relatives around. She came and sat silently in the corner of our bedroom reading a book while I literally hemorrhaged. I was so completely weak by evening that I couldn't stand alone. I needed help getting the few steps to the bathroom. And, yes, I passed tissue. Lots of it. And gray matter, too. I passed my baby, and no one in the entire world seemed to care.

You may wonder why in the world we didn't rush to the hospital for help. Truthfully, it was because we were following doctor's orders. We were too young and far too naïve at 22 to do anything different. Besides, we had an older lady with us that we trusted. I kept asking if I should be bleeding that much. She would lift her head from her book occasionally and say, "Yes." Throughout this whole ordeal I kept feeling awful for disturbing the doctor on a Sunday, and for having our friend sit with me. I felt guilty, ashamed, and a failure. Some of you may think this to be dumb, but I have talked to many, many women who have felt this same way. My body had failed, and so had I.

The heavy bleeding finally calmed down by around 11:00 p.m. Sunday night. Our friend gladly left, never to mention a word of this to us again. It was as though nothing ever happened. In the morning, I called the doctor's office. He didn't even want to see me for one week! He said, "You've probably lost the baby, but we can't be sure for several days. Just take it easy, and make an appointment to see me in a week." There wasn't even an "I'm sorry." In my heart, I already knew the baby was gone. I didn't need the doctor to confirm it.

The months that followed were some of my worst. I couldn't find any written information that really helped me to deal with how I was feeling. My husband was hurting and just remained very quiet. He hardly ever mentioned the baby. My mind was preoccupied day and night with the fact that our little baby was gone. I needed help. I didn't know that having a miscarriage was fairly common. In fact, I was convinced that I would never have another baby. No one wanted to talk, it seemed, so silent grief set in, and became a precedent for the five miscarriages that I would later experience

Many, many people would never begin to understand why anyone could cry over a baby that you have never held or never seen. Probably had I not experienced miscarriages myself, I would not understand either. A woman's body tells her very early that she is pregnant. The physical symptoms of pregnancy appear, and somehow she can almost tell that she is pregnant, even before an exam or before a pregnancy test. A woman's body begins working very hard, very fast, to prepare for the coming of this new one. I always could tell almost immediately by the swelling of my breasts, the bit of nausea, the extreme tiredness, and the way my uterus felt swollen — even a tiny bit. And these changes are exciting. Having your body prepare to nurture another body for nine months is an incredibly fascinating thought, and a wonderful, unexplainable feeling. There is a bond between mother and baby that sets in almost immediately.

The emotional ties to a baby begin immediately for most women, also. Fathers can get involved in the emotional part of early pregnancy. Do we have a little girl or a little boy? I wonder how much the baby has grown today? What has developed this week? Will the baby have a full head of hair? There is a common misconception, even today, about the emotional attachment women and men feel to this new life very, very early in pregnancy. Why do people think so many couples rush to the store to purchase a home pregnancy kit? They want to know if there really is a baby growing and developing inside. And the bond of love for so many is strong from that very moment on. There is no mistake. God made us that way. Love is like that.

There are major problems that go along with early child

loss. Many times the baby has died even before you have had time to tell others of your joy. Quite often, the support just is not there to help you through your grief and feelings of deep loss. It is an uncomfortable topic to talk about, and one that others can easily dismiss. The baby was not real to them. There will be no sympathy cards, no funeral, no real anything for this child. In many instances you will not even know if your child was a girl or boy. Personally, out of our seven losses, I know that three were girls and one was a boy. The rest of the children are "unknown." That hurts, and makes it extremely difficult to ever resolve. And so it is for so many parents.

One father went through an extremely difficult time when his wife miscarried during their third pregnancy. He came to talk to me because he knew that I had gone through child loss myself. He cried and said, "I know this one was a boy." I asked him how he knew and he said, "I just know. I just wanted a little boy so badly!" The sad thing is that he will never, ever know if the child he lost was a boy. He and his wife can only guess. In many ways, this complicates the loss. And so few people seem to understand.

While at the beach on a brief vacation this past year, I had a mother strike up a conversation with me as we were watching our children play together. After a while, she asked if she could talk to me about something personal. I laughed, and said to go ahead and ask. She wanted to know my age, and at my age, that's not really a terrific question to ask. I squeaked, rather quietly, that I was 45. She then asked how old I was when I had my youngest child. I said 43, not yet knowing what she was working towards. Then came the tears. She was extremely depressed. She had just miscarried a few weeks ago, and she and her husband were away trying to relax and come to grips with losing the baby. She said she wanted this child so badly. She was 40, and it was difficult for her to get pregnant, so she and her husband were thrilled with the news of another little one on the way.

When she went in for a routine exam, the doctor discovered there was no fetal heart beat. An ultrasound confirmed that the baby had died. She could not handle the thought of carrying a dead baby, so she had a D & C surgical procedure performed that afternoon. Gone. That quickly, it was all over. Yet, it would never be all over.

"I'm so sorry," I found myself saying. "It's too soon for you and your husband to be feeling okay, because things are not okay. You just lost a baby." She explained that people at work didn't think it was that big of a deal. They all said to hurry and get pregnant again. She was frightened. She had a difficult time conceiving. And she was 40. The odds were not stacked in her favor for having another child. Besides that, she wanted this baby.

Interestingly, her husband came over to us, as though he wanted to rescue her from me. How dare she be talking! She had explained that he had fallen into such a depression that he had spent two weeks in bed. Now he was angry and bitter. He muttered some obscenities about all people in general, as he walked away with his wife. He was mad at the world. His baby was taken away, and it wasn't fair. He was so right. It never is fair. And it hurts so very, very badly. If only others could begin to understand.

I wonder about this couple often. I wonder if they are still together. They were both grieving. She wanted and needed to talk. He needed to talk, but was so unwilling. And, more than anything, they needed to hear lots of people say, "I'm hurting with you." And then they needed people to just listen. Listen and not judge. Not tell them how it should be. Simply listen. I pray that they found listeners. People who truly cared. People who care as tenderly and gently as God cares.

Early child loss can also come in another form known as stillbirth. Simplified, this means that a baby is not born alive. In all of my years of living, I had only heard of one stillbirth, and that was a very hush-hush thing. I remember hearing how the nursery was all ready for the baby, the pregnancy was wonderful, but the baby was born dead. The mother couldn't find the strength to function, and as is the case so much of the time, the father of the baby was not even mentioned. I think that society, in general, forgets that men grieve, too. I always thought that a stillbirth would be the worst possible thing to experience. Little did I know that I would get to experience this form of child loss, too.

When I was 39 years old I was pregnant, and I was thrilled. In fact, our entire family was really excited about this baby. The older kids were old enough to know how special babies are, and the little ones couldn't wait to get their hands on a little baby.

Our dream of a large family continued to come true, despite the several miscarriages I had already gone through. When I announced this pregnancy, I found out that a close friend was pregnant and due at the same time. We had gone through a pregnancy together once before, and it was fun. We compared aches, pains, weight gain, and counted kicks. Our babies were due in July, and by mid-February we were seeing who was the biggest, and checking whose baby kicked the most.

In April my husband and I went away with our three youngest children for a few days to celebrate our anniversary. I commented on the drive that this baby must be a real sleeper. He sure wasn't as active as all of the rest. But, I had heard enough pregnancy stories by now to know that not all babies are constant kickers and movers. On our way home I really struggled to even feel a kick. I just wasn't sure any more, and I was worried. Plenty worried. These things don't happen to babies. Not at this late stage of pregnancy. And, for sure, not to my baby!

I had a doctor's appointment already scheduled for the day after we arrived home. Panic was beginning to set in, although I expressed it to no one, not even my husband. I put up a kind of mental block to protect myself from imagining that something was wrong. When I went for my exam that evening, the doctor's wife took one look at me and asked, "What's the matter? I'll go get the doctor." I must have looked terrible, and she sensed from my look that something was wrong. The doctor came at once and began searching for a fetal heartbeat, but there was none. I remember the sound of the stethoscope as it did nothing but give off a fuzzy noise, rather than the rhythmic thump of a baby's heartbeat. On the ultrasound screen, I watched with the doctor, as the baby showed no signed of life. He was dead. My baby was really dead. It was like a bad dream. A nightmare. Somehow I hoped that I would wake up the next morning and all would be well.

The rest of the evening was a total blur. I know that I had to go to the hospital for blood work. Then I went home. I still don't know how I drove the car. Shock is a weird feeling. Everything seems to move so slowly and methodically, but nothing seems to make much sense. My husband casually asked how my appointment went. I remember saying, "Not so good. The baby died." I know that he stared straight ahead, not saying a word for a long,

long time. We said we would talk about it after the kids went to bed.

For exactly two weeks and five days I carried a dead baby inside of me. My body that once held such life, held an empty shell. It is impossible to put into words what that feels like, so I will not even try. I did not know or understand all of the reasoning behind it, but it was decided to allow me to go into spontaneous labor, just as though the baby was still alive. To say I was scared was putting it mildly. Once again, I tried to get someone, anyone, to tell me what it would feel like. Nothing. No one. No answers. Only waiting. Horrid, frightened, lonely waiting.

It took my husband and me almost a week to sit the other kids down and tell them the baby had died. We needed time together to cry, and to actually believe this had happened before we could share our grief with others. The kids were amazingly wonderful, especially the younger ones. Somehow, death seemed a viable thing to them from the beginning. They told their teachers at school. "Mom's baby died." One teacher sent a letter asking why my daughter would tell such a story. The others were silent. There were no phone calls, visits, cards, or calls. But, there was avoidance.

During the weeks of carrying the baby, knowing full well that he had died, I still imagined that I felt an occasional kick. Other times I would wake up from a nightmare, imagining what the delivery would be like. I was so scared! Sometimes, I would wake up and feel my large belly and believe that I still carried a healthy, living baby. Life can be so bitterly cruel!

Telling other people of the baby's death was extremely difficult. And for the many who have gone through similar experiences, you will fully understand. I still looked quite pregnant — very pregnant. I was at the end of my 27th week when the baby died. I remember the lady at the supermarket teasing about me going into labor in the store. She asked how many more weeks I had to go, and I had to explain that the baby had died. When I told her she ran off, and she has always avoided me since. My neighbor called bubbling with excitement. "I'm having a home interior party, and they have the cutest nursery decorations. They're all new items this year. You'll love them for the baby's room." She was so upset when I told her that the baby died that she simply hung up the phone.

Telling people was horrible because I still looked fat and very pregnant. It was so difficult to say, "Our baby died in the uterus. Nobody knows why. I'm just waiting to go into delivery." Not easy, for sure. But, what is most difficult is thinking back on the silence of everyone. The silence was so loud at times that it broke my already broken heart. It still does.

I delivered a stillborn baby boy four days after Mother's Day with my husband at my side. The baby was wrapped in a little white blanket, and handed to us, for which I will be eternally grateful. My husband and I held him and counted his little fingers and toes. He was beautiful. He was real. He was our special little boy. And he was dead. I weep now eight years later as I write about him, partly because I still think of him every day, and partly because so few people seemed to even care. He was our baby. We loved him. But no one ever seemed to want to listen. It was just too difficult for them.

Since that time I have heard of one other baby dying of umbilical cord strangulation. I found very little literature to read about intra-uterine death, and even the doctors seemed not to want to talk. A reason was never given for our son's death. All that we were told was that "it was one of those things." Silence and silent grieving go hand in hand.

Parents that have lost older children may be wondering why I have spent this much time on early child loss. The reasons are obvious. Many parents grieve bitterly. They cry buckets of tears. Their hopes and dreams have been snatched away so quickly, and so many people, including those in the medical profession, do not seem to understand that it is possible to deeply love a child at 8, 12, 16, 24, and 40 weeks of pregnancy. That child is real. And the bond of love was formed.

Although during early child loss there are no memories to cause one to recall time spent together, the entire future was bitterly snatched away. Hopes and dreams of times to be spent together with this child vanished. Many parents lose three or four children in a short period of time during early pregnancy. The pain deepens with each loss, and a numbing sensation sets in.

I had a doctor tell me once when I went for a routine checkup at 14 weeks, and there was no fetal heartbeat, that "this should be old hat for you by now." His point being, I had been through it before. I remember just staring straight ahead, not looking at

````````````

that doctor, while the hot tears fell down my face. He didn't even begin to know how I felt when I heard that my baby had died. He didn't begin to say, "I'm sorry." I think that miscarriages had become so routine to him that my baby was just a number that helped prove a percentage. I never shared the news of a miscarriage with anyone after that. My husband and I grieved silently. God was our help. He always listened. He always understood. Where others were absent, He was always there.

Countless others have experienced this same lack of caring and understanding in early child loss. I pray that this book will touch each person's hurting heart, dry a tear, and help others to realize that parents do grieve early child loss, too. It is never, ever easy to lose a child.

The words "I'm sorry" can come as such a stranger in the night. Death always knocks at our door when we least expect it. All too often that's how these words do come — as strange words delivered by a stranger. There's been an accident. "I'm sorry." The child probably thought the pills were candy. "I'm sorry." He must have slipped in the bathtub and hit his head. "I'm sorry." The car took the turn too sharp, and he didn't stand a chance. "I'm sorry." The surgery went so well. We just weren't expecting this turn for the worse. "I'm sorry." Nightmare stories. Children taken so suddenly. Snatched away so quickly.

When death comes, especially the death of a child, it is never, ever the right time. That special part of you is taken away so quickly. And, no, it never seems fair. Life goes on for all of those around us, but for those who have lost a child, time just stands still. Time no longer has meaning. Nothing much has meaning. Not now.

The death of an older child, a child that has actually been a visible, feeling, talking, walking, working, part of your life, is to me, not able to be adequately put into words. The depth of pain is limitless. The child that once brought so much noise and activity, so much life to your home, is now gone. Death is so utterly, positively cruel, and it gives a cut to the heart like nothing else.

The first older child I ever knew to die was my cousin. My cousin climbed a tree in his backyard, fell out of the tree, and ruptured his spleen. He had surgery but infection set in, and at the age of 14 a once-healthy, active, super young man died. Just like that. He was gone. Since we were only a few months apart
````````````

in age, I was quite close to him. It was such a scary, strange feeling knowing that he died. For some reason my parents did not allow me to attend the funeral of my cousin, and I have always been sorry about that. It made it that much harder for me to realize that he was gone. For his parents there was total devastation to their lives. Grief held a tight grip on their hearts that lasted a lifetime. They were never completely the same again. How could they be?

We had another encounter with an older child dying when my husband and I were living in Oklahoma while he was attending college. Friends of ours lost their beautiful seven-year-old daughter to what is now known as Reyes Syndrome. She had a mild case of chicken pox and was almost recovered when she took a turn for the worse. The end result was that this precious little girl died. Her death was totally unexpected, and the pain from such a loss is inconceivable to almost any parent. I do not ever think I will forget the empty look of pain on the faces of those parents. Death is so final. So terribly final.

A mother shared the story of her little girl's battle with a terminal illness. Just battling the disease would have been pain enough for this family. As she told me of the little girl's fight for life, her whole body began to tremble. Her face tightened, and the tears fell. She came to grips with the fact that her little girl was going to die, but she said she still cannot come to grips with the absence of her friends during such a time of need. Her husband withdrew when the illness became the most severe. He just could not handle seeing the pain. As this beautiful mother shared with me her broken heart, I wanted to say something that would help. I could not say a thing that had not already been said. You see, silence of her friends spoke volumes. And still, after many years, only the tears will fall. Child loss hurts that badly.

Throughout the course of my years on this earth, I have known many, many children who have died in car accidents. Shock. Death's cold sting. So alive one minute, and so forever gone the next. I tremble at the thought of death knocking at my door this way. So totally unexpected. Our children are not supposed to die. Not this way. Not any way. Children mean life, not death. But one has only to open up a newspaper to see the harsh reality. Children die every day. And every day millions of tears are shed for those children.

Child loss is not new. It has been going on since the beginning of time. But it hurts so badly that sometimes only the tears will fall. Life loses all meaning, all purpose. Our joy is gone. We wonder if we will ever feel the same again. Only sad, empty tears fall when a child is taken away. When our child dies, part of us dies, too. Only a parent can understand that concept. So many are reluctant to share our pain, and many others are so fearful to even hear our pain, that parents are left with only silence where once there was life. And silent grief begins.

In the chapters to come, we will discuss in much greater length the depth of the loss of older children. For now, I want to say something to each and every parent who has ever lost a child. Your loss is unique. Your child was yours. There is no greater love than a parent's love for their own child. Not all people will understand your loss. Not all people will even care. Some may not even acknowledge your loss.

My advice to you is to grieve in spite of what anyone says or does not say. It is not stoic to hide your tears. It is not strength to lose all of your feelings. It is not courage to go on as though nothing at all ever happened. You have the right to hurt, and to hurt deeply. I have soaked many pillows from my tears, and I am not ashamed to say it. My husband's heart hurts, too. Let's remember that men — fathers — hurt deeply over the loss of a child. It may be a slightly different hurt than a woman feels, but it is still deep pain. Understand that it is okay to hurt. Losing a child is not an easy thing to go through. It is not a sign of weakness to grieve, as so many would try to tell us. You need your heart to be hugged, your tears to be wiped away, and a pair of listening ears. There's absolutely no shame in that.

Children, by all human reasoning, are not supposed to die before their parents. We, the parents, are supposed to grow old and die before our children. Life does not always go according to plans, though. Many times, the unexpected can happen. And when it does it knocks your feet right out from under you. When a child dies, the hurt is severe. The shock is harsh, and it is often difficult, if not impossible, to comprehend. The word "death" itself is so final. Perhaps that is the most challenging concept of all — death means absence of life. What was, is no more.

What happens when you hear those words "I'm sorry"? There is no pat answer to that question. Your reaction to the loss of your child is as individual as your child was. One common thread that all parents who have lost children share, is the common thread of pain. I have never once talked with a parent who has lost a child and heard that parent say, "I'm glad it happened." Even in the midst of a child that is suffering, we want to hold onto that child for just a moment longer. With an older person who has lived a long, fruitful life, sometimes we can be at peace when death occurs. It is difficult to see a person age, and grow increasingly more frail with each passing day. Death, in an instance such as this, brings with it somewhat of a peace. But with a child we expect life. We want life. We want our child.

Understanding the finality of the words "I'm sorry" is often the beginning of understanding that the child will no longer be here among us. There is a void that no one or nothing in this entire world can fill. I have never been an open griever. Part of the reason is that I save my most intimate feelings for those closest to me. Another reason is that grief is only multiplied when others do not understand what we are feeling. It is very, very difficult for someone who has never lost a child to begin to understand what that type of pain feels like.

So many parents have expressed this same feeling to me. One father I am thinking of in particular would not even accept condolences for his daughter's death until he heard that my husband and I had gone through several losses ourselves. He said he felt like screaming out at this daughter's funeral, "You do not know how I feel! How could you? You've never lost a child." He's right, you know. No one can completely understand this loss unless they have had their hearts touched by such an intimate walk with grief.

What has profoundly affected me lately is the fact that we live in an era of openness and honesty about so many things. Things that were once never, ever talked about. Sex is discussed openly. Divorce and single parenting no longer hold the stigma that once was held years ago. Alternate lifestyles, drugs, alcohol, teen pregnancy, and such are all talked about with a vast amount of candor. Cancer was once a hushed word. We can now say with boldness that we are battling cancer. Then there is child loss. The death of a child. A sudden hush falls over a room, twisted faces, deaf ears, and then that awful, lonely silence. Not always, but so much of the time.

In talking with parents about child loss, the overall pain that seems to be predominant is the pain of silence. Feeling so isolated. So alone. So full of loneliness, and having no real way to fill the void. I have wondered if men and women of earlier times endured child loss differently than we do today. It was very common to deliver babies at home, and have tragedies happen. One elderly woman I know told me of delivering twins in her bed alone. They were born prematurely, soon to die. Her husband was an alcoholic, her other children were too young to understand, and she had to tend to the burial herself. How did she do it? She cried. And she cried. And she cried. She got together with other ladies and they sewed, cooked, and consoled one another. They shared their feelings, and they shared their losses. Then they went on. They had to. Death was no stranger to them.

Things such as diphtheria, typhoid, polio, measles, and pneumonia claimed the lives of many children in this country not too many years ago. My own grandfather buried his first wife and all seven of his children under an oak tree on his farm. They died of the terrible influenza that claimed the lives of thousands, many of them being children. They did not have medicines like we have today to cure diseases. Parents watched painfully as many of their children died before their very eyes.

Were those people stronger, tougher in some way than we are? No, I don't think so. They simply accepted death as being more real than we do today. Did they grieve? I know that my friend who lost her twins over 60 years ago grieved for them until her death. But her strength seemed to come from being able to talk about the death of her children. At first it made me very uncomfortable to hear her talk of the babies. But as I grew to know her I learned to listen. Just listening seemed to help.

I asked my family physician, Dr. Hay, about his idea of child loss. He has been a practicing physician for many years, and has seen a great deal of changes in people and the medical profession. He began with a horse and buggy, going from house to house. Many times he battled snow-covered roads late at night. Sometimes he just didn't make it in time. Were people stronger? Maybe so. Maybe not. They were more open with their grieving, though. People gathered in the home of the one who had died, and support was given immediately. Especially when a child died. Women helped women, and the men helped the men. They talked.

They shared. They cried. They prayed. They did it together.

Maybe we are forced, to a degree, to grieve more silently today because we expect all things in life to work out. We expect medications to save children. We expect early prenatal care to assure us of a healthy baby. We expect seat belts to save lives. We expect surgeons to perform miracles. We expect bad things to happen to other people. And, when something such as a child's death occurs, our lives are totally, completely thrown off balance. We just never expect a child to die. And, for sure, we never expect *our* child to die.

When faced with those words, "I'm sorry," we need someone or something to help us get back to living again. Tears help. Tears and friends help more. Tears, friends, and listening ears are even better. Tears, friends, listening ears, and trust in God help the most.

Chapter 2

It Hurts So Badly

Everyone alive knows that people die every day. Many of us turn to the obituary section in the newspaper before reading anything else to see who has died. And we are all well aware that among those who die are children. Children of all ages. The only thing we do not realize is the intense, horrific pain that is associated with the loss of a child until . . . that loss is our child. It is at the point when the pain becomes personal that it also becomes real. When we actually taste the salty tears that come from child loss, then we become acutely aware of the pain of a broken heart. A broken life. A lost love. A forever ache. A biting sting that hurts even the very soul.

Several years ago I was teaching a class about loneliness and how loneliness affects so many people, especially during the holiday season. There were 15 ladies in the group, and I opened the lesson to discussion at the end of the session. All of a sudden, one of the ladies jumped up from her seat and ran to the bathroom sobbing. We could hear the loud sobs coming from upstairs, but not one of us went to her, I am so ashamed to say. She was crying over the death of her son which happened during the holidays a few years before. Something — probably everything — that was said that evening had vividly reminded her of her son's death. We were all in our own private world, expounding on loneliness, when we had one right among us suffering. Her heart was breaking. Not one of us, young or old, was sensitive enough to remember her in her tremendous pain. After all, it had been a couple of years since her son died. I really think we believed she should have been over the pain by now.

I cannot recall one time when I have been more bitterly ashamed of myself than at that particular moment. Not one of us went to hug this hurting woman, to hold her, or to help dry her tears. Instead, we sat staring in silence not knowing what to say. Can you believe that? We just did not know how badly it still hurt. Death, in the form of child loss, had not yet knocked at many of our doors. And death of a child had not arrived for any of us during the teen years when this woman's son died. We didn't even begin to understand her ongoing pain. And she did not understand why we did not understand. So, so sad.

Throughout the years, I have attended many funerals, the worst being those of children. There is just something so wrong about seeing a young body devoid of all life. It just was not meant to be that way. Strange as it seems, most parents go through the motions of the funeral fairly well. It has always been unimaginable to me to see a mom and dad standing beside their child's casket talking about how nice the child looks. I never really saw a dead child that looked nice. But I must understand that I have not had to go through the terrible, shocking ordeal for a long, long time. When I was at my sister's funeral, I took one look at her 13-year-old body, and she did not look nice at all to me. While my parents sat quietly, I had to be physically removed at three different times. We each handle sorrow, shock, and pain in individual ways. I still weep bitterly at a child's funeral. Children are just not supposed to die!

Shortly after the words "I'm sorry" settle in, the reality of loss hits hard. Many parents liken it to having the wind knocked out of them. They actually feel a suffocating sensation. The body and mind have almost a natural reaction to all of this pain. Shock. I truly believe that God made us this way so that we are only able to absorb small bits of such intense pain at a time. Child loss is so brutal that I do not think many parents could survive the loss without going through at least a brief period of shock. That's how they manage to go through the motions of the funeral. It is all like a dream that is playing in slow motion. It takes time for the reality to set in that it is not a dream. That's when it begins to hurt.

When I delivered our stillborn son, my sister called the hospital to see how I was doing. I talked to her, and I described in detail what our little boy looked like. I said he was perfectly formed, had a little light hair, that he had all of his fingers and toes (important to me for some reason). And then I told her how I held him for quite a while. That was it for her. She insisted I was drugged and out of my mind. I was not drugged. I had asked for no medication. I was in a mild state of shock. I was able to remain calm only because the real pain had not set in yet. In the days, weeks, and months to come the pain hit, and it hit hard. When we lose a child, we seem to go through all the motions, speak all of the right words, and then we do not remember much of anything afterward. Thank God for such a blessing. It would be too much to take in all at once.

I went to a funeral of a young boy that was killed in a car accident. Truthfully, I was dreading talking to the parents. I don't think there are very many words that can comfort or take any pain away at such a time. As it turned out, they never shed a tear. They ended up consoling me. That's what shock does. Several months later I had my chance to help them. The reality of their little boy's death had set in, and it hurt so badly. This little boy's mom went to work outside of the home, something she had not done before. She was hoping that a job would help occupy her mind. It did not. Nothing seemed to help her. She had two other children, but that did not take away the pain of the one that she lost. The family tried going away on a little vacation, just to be together and regroup their thoughts a bit. They ended up coming home early. The trip brought nothing but painful reminders to them of times spent together with their little son. He was a ball of energy, and now that enthusiasm had just left them. Nothing was the same. Just his absence at the dinner table was a daily reminder of how painful life had become. Never again would they see his smile, trip over his toys, fight with him to get a bath, or kiss him good night. Death takes so much away. The death of a child takes too much away.

In Barbara Bush's book, *A Memoir*, she goes into great detail, giving a tender account of her young daughter's losing battle with leukemia. Robin died at a young age, and with her death came much pain. Mrs. Bush gives an illustration of how terribly difficult the pain is to bear after the child you love dies. About six months after Robin died the pain of it all really set in, and night after night Mrs. Bush would wake up in actual physical pain, with her body aching and hurting all over. The pain was real. That's what child loss can do to even the strongest of us.

Many mothers that have miscarried, had a stillborn child, or lost a child in the first year of life express this same type of physical pain. The mother's arms may actually ache from wanting to hold her child so badly. The loss is felt so deeply that it even comes out in the form of physical pain. That was never explained to me by a physician, and I didn't know what my pain was. I just had no idea what was wrong. That is why I am including this section in this book for you. You are not going crazy. You are simply grieving, deeply grieving for the one you long to be with you — your child. By the way, it is not unusual for fathers to go through physical pain too, in the form of bad headaches, body aches, or unexplainable stomach aches. I wish the medical profession would tell us a bit more about this. Our not understanding what is happening to our own bodies can be terribly frightening. The pain eases with the passing of time. And the time is different for each person, so make allowances if you happen to take longer to feel better. When you have gone through something as painful as losing a child, it takes time for your mind and body to adjust. Your entire world has been torn apart, and mending is often a painful, tedious journey.

One mother wrote to me about the first year following her young daughter's death. She thought that busyness would help ease the pain. Just forcing herself to get back to work, back in the routine of everyday living. It was not that easy, though. She couldn't even remember how to set the table properly, let alone put a simple meal together. Her mind just would not work right. She could not think rational thoughts. It took her well over a year before she could get the table set and prepare a simple meal so that each food was ready at the same time. She was hurting that badly.

When a child is gone, nothing seems right anymore. Even the sunrises do not look pretty on most days. The nights are long and lonely. The house seems so empty with that one who is missing. We would do anything in the world to have that child back with us. Anything. But we know we cannot change that final blow of death. Perhaps this is why parents suffer so. Moms and dads are supposed to take care of their children. Hospitals, doctors, and nurses are supposed to know how to make them get better. And prayer. There is supposed to be such power in prayer. Wasn't God listening? Our minds are left with painful, often angry questions of hurt. The only thing we know for sure is that our child is never coming back. That hurts like nothing else in the world.

I visited with a mother whose teenage son was quite unexpectedly killed in a car accident. It was late in the day when I went to see her, and she was still in her night clothes. She had such a blank, empty stare coming from her eyes. She could not focus on anything, she explained. Getting dressed was her biggest chore of the day. She had no desire to get up from bed, put on her clothes, or to comb her hair, much less do anything else. She had lost her youngest son, and with that loss went the meaning for all of life for her. At least for now.

Her husband came into the house, and he was deep in grief, too. He said he just mowed the lawn over and over. That was his time alone just to think. He said that everything was a constant reminder of their son — the garage where they worked together, the yard where they had played ball. The grass that he mowed had been his son's job for years. And then he just put his face into his hands and sobbed.

The aftermath of the words "I'm sorry" is like the aftermath of a tornado. There is total, unexpected devastation, hearts hewn down to rubble. Brokenness. Hurt. Awful, nagging pain that just will not seem to go away. And the reminders. Those constant reminders. Every lady that has lost a baby in early child loss can probably identify with this one. Every place that you go, and I do mean every place, you will see round bellies and happy faces. After the loss of one of my children at 16 weeks of pregnancy, I had to go to the hospital for follow-up blood work. I counted 12 very pregnant women there during that brief period of time. Every round-bellied woman I saw was a reminder of my loss. And it hurt so badly. I wanted to run down the corridor to get out of that place as quickly as I could. I didn't need those visible reminders. Not right then. Not ever. No parent ever wants those painful reminders of what you have lost. But they are there. Everywhere.

The mother who has had a baby that died shortly after birth

will be bombarded by mail, phone calls, advertisements, and offers for free gifts, all for new babies. All cruel, cruel reminders of the loss. Your world has been shattered, torn apart. And others don't even know. Life just seems to go on as usual, despite your pain.

About two months after the loss of our stillborn son, my husband and I felt the need to just go out alone for an hour. So we went someplace nearby to eat, and sat a table far away from all others. We really didn't feel like being around anyone. We were just beginning to get beyond the constant tears, but our hearts were still heavy. About halfway through our meal a young couple decided to sit in an empty booth not three feet away from us. Of course they had a tiny baby boy in an infant carrier that they sat right down in the aisle by us. They were so proud of their little boy; we were so grieved over the loss of ours. Our meal was over. It just hurt too much. Any parent who has suffered this loss knows exactly what I am talking about. You want to be happy for others and share in their joy. You see the excitement on their faces as they show off their new little bundle. But you just don't feel like you can be happy for them. Not yet. It's just too soon.

There just seems to be no escape from the painful reminders of the loss of your child. Maybe it's a special song that comes on the radio, or a silly saying that you shared with your child. Maybe a certain smell serves as a reminder of a special moment or tender occasion with your child. A certain smile. A stuffed teddy bear. The list could go on and on, and is uniquely different for each child that has died. Each child had special qualities, those special moments that made your relationship special. If your loss was early, then you held special expectations, special hopes with that child. Now those hopes are gone, as though they never even existed. When that circle of love is broken by absence, it hurts so much. Never again will a meal or a family gathering be the same. Not when your special someone, your special child is missing. And no one really, truly comprehends this type of lonely pain until that pain personally touches your own heart.

When I was 15 years old, my 13-year-old sister died. She had been living away in a home for the terminally ill for the last six months of her life. We were only two years apart in age, but no one told me that she was going to die. I thought she was living away to get better. When she died, I thought I had died, too. It has been 31 years now since her death, and I can recall every detail of being told what happened on that horrible day of June 6.

I did not have a guidebook for grief, and no one sat down and talked with me about her death — ever. My mother and father divorced, so there was no real warm, close family relationship after her death. Only lonely reminders of how things used to be.

One day I found a bag of my sister's clothes hidden away in a back closet of our home. It was so great to take out each dress and look and remember. I guess that's the difference between a parent's loss and a sibling's loss. I wanted, I needed, to remember. My mother wanted no reminders. I didn't know this, so I took one of those dresses from the bag and put it on my younger sister. What a dreadful mistake! I can still hear my mother screaming when she saw that dress on my little sister. I really think she hated me at that moment. There is such a fine line between deep grief and hatred.

The dresses were not just packed away this time. They were burned. But, even as the dresses burned, the memories of a feisty, 13 year old were left behind. There just is no escape, just pain. Every parent who has ever suffered child loss will tell you this. Memories can be wonderful, but early on they serve as constant, daily, hourly reminders of what you no longer have. Your child. Your precious child. Your child is gone.

A few years back we had a frightening experience with our then three-year-old son Marc. I was holding Marc, reading to him, and as I touched his bony arms I felt lumps. Several lumps. They were all over his body. My mind went crazy with fear. I grabbed my trusty medical book, and nothing I read sounded good. It would be several hours until morning when I could call the doctor. It was a frightening night of waiting, and a worse day to come.

Dr. Hay wanted to see Marc immediately. He didn't like what he felt at all. The lumps were there. It was not my imagination. I was sent immediately to another doctor; from there to the hospital for a series of tests. We would have to wait until morning to know if he had leukemia.

Since I had already known of children with leukemia, my mind went wild. I told my husband the minute he walked through the door of the doctor's suspicions, and we called the other kids together to let them know that Marc might be real sick. I was crying already. I was trying to imagine the future without Marc, and it hurt just to think about it for even a minute. Our 15-year-old son ran and locked himself in the bathroom crying. The other kids didn't want Marc to go to bed. They needed to play with him. He made awful, loud car noises as he pushed his little toy cars and trucks across the floor. Those noises used to drive us all crazy. Not now. We all sat and cried as he hummed, purred, and pushed those silly cars around. We missed him already, and he was still with us. We didn't know how we would ever live in this old house any more without his car noises.

Death did not knock at our door that time. Marc had to have a year of antibiotics and then his tonsils removed and some ear surgery. As I am writing at this moment, Marc is almost ten years old, and you guessed it. He's pushing a truck around me making his famous noises.

Why did I even go into this story if Marc is okay? Many of you were not so lucky with the outcome of your child's tests. Your child did have leukemia. Your child did have bone cancer. Your child lost the battle. Your child died. And so did your child's special noises. I can only say that for a brief 24-hour period of time our family lived with a hint of what many of you must live with each day. Those brief hours of pain changed us — all of us — forever. I never complained about those noises again. I love hearing them! Many people don't know how my husband and I can tolerate the noise, the mess, the constancy of having the little ones around us. That one very brief glimpse into your corner, those of you who have had to face the death of a young child, changed us. There is no silence, no grief, no pain such as that which comes with the death of a child.

My heart hurts for every parent, every home, that has to endure such loss. There is no pill, no drink, no work, no anything that can make it feel better. Not at this point, anyway. And so few people seem to understand.

We have not really talked about losing adult children yet, and that must be included in child loss. Marvelous happenings occur between parents and children after the young, dependent years, and then the often-turbulent teen years. As our teens mature into adults they take on a new role in our lives. They become our friends, many times our best friends. My husband and I are blessed with some adult children right now, and it is a wonderful, happy relationship. We look forward to our phone conversations, and visits are anticipated with enthusiasm beyond belief. They are our children, our friends. Our love has grown even deeper and stronger for them. As our children grow older, that bond of love grows stronger and stronger.

I have a dear friend, an older lady, who lost her son a few years ago to a terrible accident. This death was swift and so unexpected. He left behind a wife and three beautiful children. The young man's family pulled together and began to adjust after a year of his death. But not his mother. She had lost a young child to miscarriage. She is now widowed. She lost both of her parents. Why such grief over this adult son? The son had a family of his own now. He had not lived with his mother for years. And yet she is in such grief. I couldn't understand. She said quite simply one day, "I lost my son, my best friend." They had a wonderful relationship.

This mother said it all. When our children grow up they become our close friends. We've nursed them through chicken pox, colds, broken legs. We've cheered them on in basketball and baseball. We've struggled with them through all of the adventures of school. We have shared volumes of life's moments together. And when that adult child of ours dies, all of that sharing is gone, too. Such a large chunk of our life has been snatched away, and just when we were beginning to enjoy it so.

My own grandmother suffered this type of loss. Within one year she had two of her three adult children die. One of those children was my mother. My grandmother said to me that's the worse kind of loss you can feel. She loved her children. They visited her. They cared for her. They were company for her. They were her life. And when they died, a large part of her went with them. She is in a nursing home now, but guess who she calls out for? Her children that are gone. It is an ache, a pain that just never goes away at any age.

A very dear friend of my family, Doug Lawyer, lost his only son to leukemia many years ago. Doug has always talked about his "precious little Dougie boy" quite openly. He says it has helped in his grieving to keep his little Doug's memory alive. In talking with Doug, I asked him if time truly heals the hurts, or if one merely learns to live with time. Doug, in his wisdom and love, shared with me that the passage of time helps in that it gives you new perspectives on life. And with the passage of time comes the longing to be with your child even more. Doug openly shared with me that even after many years since his son's death, he still weeps when certain songs play on the radio or when he sees a child's smile that reminds him of his little Doug. He said that for him and his wife, it's a pain that never truly goes away. There will always be a corner of the heart that never completely closes itself off to the pain of losing a child — your child. Somehow, the pain of child loss always manages to stay with you forever.

During this period of time following those life-changing words "I'm sorry," parents are forced to go through tremendous changes. Changes they never asked for. Changes they never expected. And changes they never, ever wanted. Losing a child forces a parent into a realm of pain. And I have never met a person yet who welcomes pain. Not that kind of pain.

Parents begin a journey, a lonely trek to find the way back from the outside world of pain and throbbing hurt, to a place where life can at least feel reasonable. This journey is called grief. The intense grief following the loss of a child can be almost paralyzing. When we are forced to live in a new world, a world of hurt, it is not a welcome world and we often resist.

There is a young lady I know who miscarried during her fourth month of pregnancy. The shock, the hurt, the disbelief of it all has been at times almost too much. Since this happened over three years ago, even her family seems tired of her grief. But you must understand, we all must understand, that grief has no timetable to follow. She is still hurting so badly from this loss that even the sight of a baby turns her to tears. She's trying. She really is. It's just taking longer for her than most people would expect. Should we expect — do we have the right to expect — her, or anyone, to fit into our timetable for grief? Grief takes time. Pain from child loss is unavoidable. And each individual suffers in intensity unique only to that person. Each person must have his individual time to grieve.

During this period of time when nothing seems to make much sense, if any sense, many husbands and wives begin to pull away from each other. Pain brings questioning. Questions often bring doubt. And doubt certainly intensifies guilt. Some sources say that 90 percent of all marriages end when a child dies of terminal illness. That is a significant figure. What that means is that many parents just hurt so much that they never pull out of the hurt — not together.

When preparing this book I had the help of many, many parents from all over this country. Many freely helped; very many were reluctant. They were just hurting too badly yet. I repeatedly asked one question to parents who have suffered child loss, and nine out of ten times the parents chose not to answer the question. That question was, "Did you openly grieve for the loss of your child together, as husband and wife?" It is a question that hurts. When two people are hurting so badly, one of two things happens. They either are drawn closer together or they close out each other to their pain. More often than not they shut each other out. This has always bothered me, especially seeing firsthand what it did to my parents. We do not know how to share our grief. Besides that, it is much easier to push a person away and not let them into that private, hurting part of our life. For a husband and wife who together have lost a child, this silent grief can be the beginning of the end of the marriage. It is a serious matter to consider.

For those who have had to deal with the long process of the terminal illness of a child, grieving sets in before the actual death. And, no, even though you are told that your child will inevitably die, you can never be fully prepared for the pain that accompanies death. As long as there is life, there is a flicker of hope. When life ends, there is no hope left of that child getting well again. As my own parents hurt deeper and deeper about the inevitable death of my sister, they grew further and further apart. They fought. They placed blame. They suffered from guilt. They became angry. They felt helpless. And they grieved apart from one another. Their separateness had become so bitter by the time of her death that neither one of them spoke a word to each other through the viewing, the funeral service, and the burial of my sister. They even rode in separate cars to the memorial service. This was their child, their gift of love, and deep grief had crossed the line to bitter hate. It was not until I was much older that I could even begin to understand how badly they each hurt. They needed each other so. But it was easier, less painful to turn away.

I have known countless other couples who have had this very thing happen, and it saddens me deeply. The pain of loss just becomes intensified when a husband and wife cannot grieve together.

I was talking to a young couple about the death of their first child who was born prematurely. He only lived a short while in the hospital, then died. They had a funeral service for this precious baby, and it was heartbreaking. They have since had three other children and I asked them what helped them through that first year after the baby's death. They seemed to have adjusted so well. This couple became quite tense and uncomfortable at my question, so I changed the subject. I knew that all was not well.

About a month later I received a call from the husband explaining why they became so upset. He said, "We've never discussed the baby since the day of the funeral. I really don't know how my wife feels. The doctor said to hurry and try to have another baby, so that's what we did."

I was amazed. I told him I was a bit surprised to hear this. I couldn't believe that they never cried, never talked, never got angry, never did anything "together" over the death of this baby. His answer was simple. "It just hurt too much to talk about it."

Since child loss throws life so out of kilter, so totally out of perspective, it is only natural to assume that the husband/wife relationship will in some way suffer. Men see things differently than women, and they show their pain in different ways. Women have not just the emotional bond of the child to deal with, but the physical attachment as well. Couples so often misinterpret their feelings because they do not think the same way. And, for sure, grieving parents do not think the same way.

A woman that miscarries has her body to contend with, as well as her mind. Hormones are racing wildly. A body that was in full swing preparing for a birth, does a quick reversal and now changes back to an unpregnant state. Mood swings are common. Outbursts of tears for no reason occur at any time. There may be uncontrolled fits of anger about the failure of her body. A woman may have a lack of wanting to be physically near her husband. She doesn't want her body to be touched, invaded again. Not yet. These are all normal feelings, quite normal. They will not last forever. But if a husband does not know this, he will certainly misinterpret these things. And probably wrongfully criticize and judge his wife. All she is doing is adjusting to her intense grief.

A man may become overly quiet, not wanting to share his true feelings. After all, men aren't supposed to cry. That would only make him feel more weak than he already feels. A man may throw himself wildly into his work just to avoid his feelings for a time. He also may want physical intimacy with his wife more than ever now. He needs to feel close to someone. If a woman, a grieving woman, does not understand these things, she will certainly misinterpret her husband's actions. Their lack of communication during this bitter period of grief only adds to their grief. And, if communication was poor between the husband and wife before the death of a child, this terrible loss certainly will not help to bring a couple closer to one another.

May I interject something here that many, many people may never even think about? We have been taught to believe that clergymen, doctors, surgeons, psychologists, counselors, teachers, attorneys, nurses, and such are here to help us. And they are. What we must understand as fellow sufferers is that pain hurts all people. A doctor that loses a child suffers the same deep pain as any other parent that loses a child. A minister feels deep grief at the loss of a child, just as much as any other parent. Maybe these servants suffer an even deeper grief at times because they have failed to save their own. Hold on to that thought because it may help us later on in this book.

A couple that I have known for many years suffered the loss of a child early in their marriage. The father has always been an outgoing person, a real talker. The mother has always been more reserved with her feelings. They have grieved quite, quite differently, but because of their wisdom they have made allowances for each other and were able to remain strong in their love for one another. He talked and talked and talked at work about the child's death. Yes. He knew it made others feel uncomfortable. But he hurt so badly that he needed to talk. His wife, on the other hand, almost became a recluse for a while, totally depending on the strength of her husband. He held her as she cried and cried. He made allowances for her moods. He moved along in his grief, not in his pain, a bit sooner than his wife. But he held her up for years when she could not stand alone. Never once did

I ever hear him say a disparaging word about her. His love and patience were unending. They have held a beautiful marriage together, and their love is stronger because of this deep loss. When it hurt so, so badly, the husband was needed by his wife, and she was wise enough to allow him to help. Together they suffered. Together they hurt. Together they continue to grow in their love.

I wish all stories had a happy ending like the one above, but we often do everything humanly possible to avoid pain. Husbands and wives, so in need of one another's close, intimate, tender love, often turn on each other. They become bitter reminders of the past. Remember earlier when I said my mother looked at me with hate? Bitter, bitter grief can do that, especially between a husband and a wife.

I urge all couples to talk of their grief together. Hold tenaciously onto one another, even when you don't want to. When it hurts so, so badly — say so. Ask your husband or wife for help. The help is usually there. It may be painfully awkward at first. Usually baring our true feelings to anyone is painful. But in the case of a married couple, you need to be pulling together, lifting one another up, not separating and pushing each other away.

After my first miscarriage I didn't know what I was feeling, much less what my husband felt. So silence crept into our lives. Days went by when we didn't speak. We just couldn't. Often, after he left for work, I would just sit on the floor and cry all day. My emotions were running wild, and I had no one to share those feelings with. It just seemed like my husband didn't even care that we lost a baby.

Several weeks after our loss, I had been crying more than usual, and my husband fixed me a meal. I can still see it, smell it, and taste it. The pages on which I'm writing are wet with tears as I remember his tenderness. He fixed me a baked potato, a small steak, and baby buttered carrots. He brought the meal to me on a tray and served me in bed. But, before beginning the meal, he took my hand, looked into my eyes, and gently said, "I love you, and I hurt so badly, too. I just don't know what to do." We ate that meal through salty tears, and that moment sealed our marriage forever.

I share this with you only to say that it is terribly difficult for couples who are grieving the loss of a child, their child, to express their feelings to each other. We often become so weighed down in our own grief that we cannot see the grief of the person who intimately shared our child's life. It hurts so, so badly, and it is so difficult.

At some time during this period of hurting, the "why" question seems to silently creep into our hearts, and if left to grow can destroy us. Why does a child have to die? Why did our child have to die? Why such a tragic death? Why such a painful death? Why did our child die so unexpectedly? Why — when only two seconds could have meant the difference between life and death in the accident? Why?

One mother shared with me her story of three consecutive child losses. She had trouble conceiving, which made her pain even greater. It seemed her sisters had babies with no problems, but not her. It took four years of trying to conceive. At 12 weeks she lost the first baby. The pain was severe, but bearable. She hoped and longed for another child one day. Two years later she was pregnant and overjoyed. This time, she carried to 16 weeks, then lost the baby. Bitter tears flowed this time. She and her husband so counted on this baby. Once again she and her husband were blessed with a pregnancy after four years of trying. This was it. She knew it, and praise was given to God. Then, unexpectedly, at the end of her seventh month she delivered a stillborn son. My heart ached for this beautiful woman as she told me of such private moments in her life.

For the first time in her Christian life, she grew angry with God. She said it was almost like being taunted with the idea of having a child, only to have each baby unexpectedly snatched away. She no longer sang praises to God; she cried bitter, bitter tears. I asked how her husband held up through all of this, and the tears ran down her face. "He was wonderful. He was my strength." Unknown to her, he kept a daily journal of his feelings, hurts, and pain. That was his way of dealing with the grief. He also was able to hold fast to God when she could not. The pain was just too much.

Did her husband understand? Yes. He tenderly walked her down the path of pain. Did God understand her questions, her tears, her crying out, and even her anger? I would have to say yes. He understood Job in all of his questioning. He understood the bitter cries of the shepherd David. Grief and hate have a fine dividing line. Husbands and wives need to share their grief with each other and keep each other from crossing over that fine line.

This lady's story ended happily, by the way. Just two years ago she became pregnant again. This time she was gripped with fear and hardened with anger. She said she did not allow herself one moment of joy throughout the entire pregnancy. She was just too afraid to hope again. Some would criticize her for this. I would say she needed compassion and understanding. She had been through a lot of pain. At the end of nine months she did deliver a perfectly healthy baby boy, and she did come back to God again.

Why did she and her husband have to walk this long journey of pain and tears? No one knows. She knows that the pain was awful. She would never want to go through it again. It still hurts so much that she cried often as she told me of her story. Her heart will never be the same. Neither will her husband's heart. Neither will their relationship. Fortunately, they held onto each other. And even through periods of anger they were able to keep God near.

Not every couple is able to share their grief with each other. Instead, anger, bitterness, guilt, and resentment take over where love once was. And the pain of child loss is multiplied. In the coming chapters we will discuss ways to avoid these harmful feelings, and learn how to grow closer together.

For now, probably the most important thing to remember is that the pain from child loss is like no other pain around. It is normal to do or say the abnormal for a while. What you have gone through has not just been an interruption in your life, but has turned your whole world inside out and upside-down.

When the reality sets in that your child is really and truly gone, it is normal to feel dark and sad. As you watch others go about their daily lives, you may even resent them for not seeming to care about your new, meaningless world. Just remember two things. You are never totally alone. And one day you *will* feel better. It takes time to adjust to pain. Sometimes it takes lots of time. Don't try to rush yourself, despite the urgings of others. After all, you have to live with the loss — others don't. They can walk away.

Do not expect others to fully understand what you are feeling. They cannot feel the pain of losing your child to the degree that you feel the pain. It is just not possible. To expect that kind of empathy is expecting next to the impossible, and places extreme burdens and guilt on everyone.

For husbands and wives, force yourselves to turn to each other. To turn away from each other only adds to the burden you are already carrying. This child was yours. A shared part of you is now gone. Share your hurt, too. Realize that you will each suffer a bit differently. God made men and women different in many ways, especially in our thinking and feelings. Help one another; don't add to each other's deep, deep pain.

When your hurt becomes unbearable, allow the tears to fall freely. Do not pass judgment for those who may ask the question "why." Why is a good question, but one that will never fully be answered. Not in this life. When you feel anger building up inside of you, let it go. Anger will do you no good. Allow space and time for personal grief, but draw close to your mate during your times of deepest grief. You lost your child; learn to hurt together over this child.

And in your times of deep, deep hurt, turn always to God. We often turn our faces away from Him, too, especially during our periods of questioning. He is there. He is waiting to help. And He will help you through those times that are unbearable. In asking parents of all walks what the number one thing was that helped them through the initial intense pain of child loss, there is a resounding answer. Prayer! God's love is strong. He is sure. He understands. Let Him into your broken heart. He is the only one that can truly understand.

Chapter 3

"Where Are My Friends?"

No one cares for my soul (Ps. 142:4).

Friends are great people. And most of us have a group of people that we consider to be our close and dear friends. We go to dinner together. We attend ball games together. We go shopping together. We get together for an evening of laughter and activities. We attend church services together, as well as potluck dinners and picnics. It is just plain fun to spend time with friends. Even as I am writing this, I must stop to meditate for a while, thinking of all of the many fun times shared with friends. There is just nothing quite like that type of relationship aside from the relationship found in a close-knit family. And often, because of conflicts of interest or severed ties from years past, our friends fill in that void that was once occupied by our family. Friends are cherished and friends are wonderful. We can openly and honestly be ourselves around our true friends and not have to put on any false pretenses or be afraid to just plain be our real, imperfect selves. Friends allow us room to breathe, allow us to let our hair down, and allow us to show our not-so-lovely side. Where others would pass judgment or criticize, friends understand and overlook.

When a child dies, something very strange happens to a friendship. I believe that I have heard this thought expressed to me hundreds of times now. I know that I have felt the sting of this change in friendship personally several times. When a child dies, most friends make themselves scarce in a very brief period of time. Friendships that were once so close become somewhat strained. People who were open and honest with their feelings now find it difficult to carry on a simple conversation. The air is cool; the talk is forced and so surface. The words just do not seem to flow freely anymore. Permanent changes occur in the lives of those who lose a child, and many friends cannot deal with these changes. It is just easier to stay away from a grieving parent. This statement is not meant to hurt, but to help a hurting parent understand. It has taken me literally years to understand this different behavior in friendships. I now understand, but I also believe that we need a great deal of help in this particular area of friendships. Losing friends causes a feeling of deep rejection. And rejection by those who were once so close to us is the last thing a grieving parent needs.

When a child first dies, or a life ends due to a miscarriage or stillbirth, most friends are supportive. Your home is filled with the aroma of all kinds of delicious food to help you through those difficult first few days ahead. Your mailbox may be jammed full of cards, notes, and expressions of sympathy. Your home often becomes a constant place of noise from friends stopping by to say how sorry they are for you and your family. Your telephone may ring endlessly with shocked, hurt, sympathizing friends. This is wonderful, and is the main source that sustains you through the first few difficult days and weeks after your child has died. It is so nice, so comforting, to know that people, our friends, do truly care.

After about a month though, the dust seems to settle and so do our friends. When we lose a child, whether that child was ten weeks into a pregnancy, ten years old, twenty years old, or more, the bite of death reaches through to the very center of our being — our heart. And that bite hurts like nothing else on the face of this earth. Everything around us seems to be tinted with the unlovely color of black. We can talk to ourselves, trying to convince our minds that we can, we must, go on in our living. But that awful black seems to seep through every crack and crevice of our lives. This is only natural. So much sunshine has been taken away from us.

The death of a child literally takes away a real part of a parent's life. It leaves a void that cannot be filled. The small, simple things like eating a meal, driving to the grocery store, getting dressed for the day, become such enormous chores. During this settling period, as we will call it, we realize that our child's death is real. It is not a dream that will one day allow us to wake up and find that everything is happy, well, and back to normal. Our child is gone from this life. Forever. The one we loved is no longer here, and no one or nothing is ever going to change that one harsh, unbearable fact. I find myself hurting even as I am writing about the pain which accompanies losing a child. Even my breathing has changed. It is shallow and tense. My head hurts, and my eyes are dripping hot tears. Every parent who has ever had a child die understands exactly what I am talking about. The fact that our child's death means a final separation from us on this earth is a painful thought. And it hurts so badly that our vision of everything in life becomes cloudy and dark. This is the time that we most need the faithful help of a friend.

A young man came to me not long ago and wanted to know if he could talk. He had suffered a severe loss, and it was now eight months since his child died of a terminal illness. His eyes filled with tears as he tenderly told of caring for his daughter. He considered it a privilege to be able to be near her during that final, painful month before she died. Right after her death he was flooded with friends by his side. But now it is a different story. He said that he has never felt so alone in all his life. He asked that heartbreaking question, "Where are my friends?" He explained how he has tried time and time again to talk at work to his friends, but only silence echoes in his ears. He said that he tries not to cry, but every now and then he finds himself unable to hold back the tears. His friends walk away when this happens until he gains control of his emotions. His story of heartache and loneliness lasted for three hours, and I was left hurting so very much for this young man — someone my family only knows casually.

I must confess, I did not have any great words of wisdom to impart. Where child loss is involved, I do not believe that there are any real solid words to take away the pain. Words provide very little comfort when a child dies. And words never, ever begin to take the deep, inner hurt away. But I had two ears that listened, and tear ducts that opened up quite freely with this man. I then asked if he would like to join our family for pizza one night. At that suggestion he got up from his chair, put his head on my shoulder, and sobbed. "I'd love that. I can't tell you how much I would love that." My family did enjoy a meal together with this young man since that first talk. In fact, we have shared several meals and several talks since that time. And there will be more. You see, the holidays are approaching and he needs friends to see him through. No. He is not always cheerful to be around. Sometimes tears fall onto his plate while he is eating. Many times he sits, staring, totally silent. I would imagine the pain hurts so much that if he ever let loose, he could fill buckets with his tears. He misses that one that meant the world to him. Every single day there is something to remind him of his loss. "Men are supposed to be strong," he said. "And sometimes I really feel like I am just not going to make it."

How I wish that tears were not associated with weakness! Where did we ever learn that crying means we are weak? This man needs more than an occasional card or a weak "How are you?" asked in casual conversation. He needs the constant, continuous help of friends. A friend. Any one who will help him get back up again and put some color into his life. Every person alive needs a friend. Every parent who has lost a child needs a close friend. A faithful friend. A friend who will just be there.

I met with a nurse as this book was coming into being, and I asked her several difficult questions about child loss. One question that I asked was why the medical profession is not more friendly, more helpful, to parents who have gone through the pain of child loss. I realize that there are some doctors and professionals who are very helpful, but in the questions that I repeatedly asked parents I received an overwhelming message that more help was needed in this area. This nurse was quick to answer. She did not even hesitate one bit. "It is too gruesome. We like to heal people. And when we cannot come out winners, we try to quickly shut down that feeling of failure." Then she went on to explain that if a doctor or nurse extends too much friendship, that involves time. And, friendship also involves listening. Both time and listening are a mental and physical drain. She was so very right, and I disagree with her philosophy of detachment so very much. A parent going through the tormenting pain of child loss needs friends. A friend is so much better than the quick fix of a pill or a bottle of alcohol that only numbs for a brief while. Often, just two simple words, "I'm sorry," accompanied by five minutes of time can do a lot to comfort. Parents are left wondering, "Where, oh where, are my friends?" Doctors and nurses are needed to be friends during child loss. They tend well to the physical needs of a parent, but the mental needs are often left unattended. Parents who have lost a child need friends. How unfortunate, how very sad, that more in the medical profession do not see this tremendous need.

I will never, ever forget the lack of friendship shown to me after the loss of one of my children. I was four months pregnant when I lost the baby. I asked the doctor, "Do you know if it was a boy or a girl?" A legitimate question to ask, I thought. He snapped at me as he was walking out of the door, "I don't know. It was just a mass of tissue." I felt like screaming back at him. "That was not a mass of tissue. That was my baby, and I would like to know just a little bit more about my child." I thought that I deserved a much kinder response than I got. Yes, I understand professional detachment. No. I do not understand professional unkindness. I needed a friend. Five minutes is all it would have taken to explain that the baby was not developed enough to identify whether I had lost a little girl or a little boy. Five minutes and a little kindness. Instead, I was made to feel like an intruder who interrupted a good night's sleep. Many, many of you can personally identify with this very type of mistreatment.

When I was 26, I had three children and had gone through one early miscarriage. The pain of that first loss was still there, along with the fear that this could happen again. Always wanting a large family, my husband and I hoped for another child, and we were blessed with a pregnancy and all of the excitement that comes with the thoughts of a new life. By November I was 18 weeks into the pregnancy and beginning to really bulge at the tummy. However, I began some intermittent spotting, and knew that this was not a good sign. My doctor examined me, and all seemed well. The baby was growing. There was a strong fetal heartbeat. I was in excellent health. So I was told to rest and stay off of my feet as much as possible for the next few days. About a week later, in mid-afternoon, with absolutely no warning, I began to hemorrhage. Thankfully, my husband was home and we only lived a block away from the hospital. The bleeding was frightening and I was already tense and crying, knowing what was about to happen.

The next few hours remain a nightmarish blur. An emergency D & C surgical procedure was performed to stop the bleeding and to remove all remaining fetal tissue. By 7:00 p.m. that evening I was out of the recovery room and it was all over. The baby, our baby, was gone. A little life ended.

Two things stand out in my mind about this loss, and although it has been 20 years since this occurred, I still have occasional tears and bad days from the loss of this baby. I cried very quietly in the hospital room as a nurse was taking my blood pressure. I really did want this baby, and had formed quite an attachment already. This loss seemed to hit me hard and fast. The nurse asked me a question. "Do you have any other children?"

I answered, "Yes. I have three."

Then she so abruptly said, "Stop your crying. You are acting like this is the end of the world. Some women never even have one baby." She was right telling me not to pity myself, but the timing was so, so wrong. So terribly wrong. I used to see that nurse quite often in our small town, and I never forgot her. I never will. I needed a friend — even for a brief moment. But, she just did not want to be bothered. Besides that, because of me she had to stay an extra half-hour on her shift. If only she had been a friend. Just for a few minutes.

The other thing that I remember is our church's New Year's Eve party that year. My husband was the minister, and neither one of us felt like going to a party, but the pressure was on to go celebrate the coming in of a new year. My husband has always been somewhat of a cutup, and he is known to liven up any party. I thought, maybe, just maybe, being around friends would help. So we went to the party and as it turned out it was a total disaster. The more the evening went on, the more sad I became. I guess the fact finally seemed real that the new year would not bring a new baby into my arms.

No one really talked to me much that evening. I now know why. I made everyone feel too uncomfortable. No one knew what to say, so nothing was said. Except — a close, close friend of ours came over to the chair where I was sitting, and he told me just how things should be. "We're getting tired of seeing you acting so down. Get with it. This is a party. So, celebrate! You're no fun to be around any more." I felt my eyes filling, so I ran upstairs to the bathroom and locked the door. I grabbed a towel and sobbed into it, and then kept splashing my face with cold water to help my red, puffy eyes look a little normal. These were my closest friends. They didn't even begin to understand how my husband and I felt. We had just lost a baby. We did not feel like celebrating the new year just yet. A new life was taken so abruptly from us. A life that we wanted. A life that we so dearly loved. My husband and I were hurting, and our friends were looking to us to be the life of the party. They were right. We were not much fun to be around that evening. But they were so terribly wrong in looking to us for strength during our time of weakness. We were left asking the question, "Where are my friends?"

In talking to a mother who lost her young four-year-old daughter to a rare genetic disease, she went on and on at length about friends. She and her husband had what she considered to be hundreds of friends — good, close, warm friends. But, something terrible happened when her little daughter died. For a few weeks after her daughter's death she was literally bombarded by calls, visits, cards, and food. These things seem to be the traditional grief helps that we do for our friends. But then she said that everything seemed to come to an immediate halt. A silence set in. The support was gone. Invitations to go to dinner, to do anything normal, stopped. Even her husband abandoned ship, which made the pain of losing her little girl even more excruciating. Her husband found that it is not much fun to be around a wife who cries a lot, who cannot get moving in the morning, who cannot entertain guests, and who could not be physically intimate with him just yet. So he left. He held true to the statistics. The pain of it all was just too much.

This lady even felt abandoned by her minister. She needed "presence," not the quoting of Scriptures. She needed to be drawn nearer to her friends, not put at arm's length because she was too gloomy to be around. She needed someone to listen to her, not someone telling her just how things should be. She needed to be held up and walked through the aftermath of the valley of death, not told to climb a mountain and reach for the stars. She needed someone, any one of her many friends, to help pull her and her husband together. She did not need the whisperers who talked about the sordid affair that followed their little girl's death. She needed someone to hold her shaking hands and help steady them, not someone to tell her how to busy her hands with work. She needed someone to stay by her side until the dust of death settled. She needed a friend. Instead, she was left alone in her grief, asking that awful, burning question, "Where are my friends?"

I received a letter a few weeks ago stating simply, "I am deep in grief. I need a friend. I never knew that someone could so easily be forgotten by everyone." My heart chords were pulled tight. I felt ashamed. I, too, had forgotten my friend in her need. And I made the false assumption that other friends and family were tending to her needs. How wrong I was! I called her immediately and we made plans to go out to eat. To be perfectly honest, I did not look forward to our time together. Who wants to listen for hours to another's pain, and not really know what to say? This woman lost her teenage son almost two years ago, and somehow it was assumed that by now she and her husband should be getting their lives back together. They are not. Far from it. The grief is much deeper now than it was a year ago. That's how grief usually works. It deepens with time. Yes. She is getting counseling. Yes. She does attend support group meetings. But throughout the course of the evening she explained that counseling and help groups are not the same as talking to a close friend — someone who knows you from way back when. She needed to talk with someone who personally knew her son. Someone who knows her husband, too.

As we talked, we recalled many happy times together. We talked about being pregnant together. The only difference is that I still have my son; she does not. The shame that fell over me was burdensome. I had been like all the others. I had left my friend during her worst time of need. Our evening together turned out to be one of the best evenings I have ever enjoyed with a friend. And, believe it or not, we mostly laughed. She needed to hear fond remembrances of her son. Her sadness was lifted, if only momentarily. She needed the touch, the very presence of a friend. And she and her husband will need the loving touch of friends for a long time to come.

Seven years ago my oldest daughter delivered a son almost

eight weeks prematurely. While in labor, Michelle had to be life-flighted to a much larger hospital than our local one, with a neo-natal intensive care unit. Jonathan was born prematurely, but with very few complications as compared to so many of the other little babies in the unit. The hospital where Jonathan was born is quite large, and the preemie ICU was full of tiny babies strug-gling to hold on to life. One thing struck me as so terribly odd, almost eerie. There was such a quietness in that unit. Moms and dads came to visit their babies hanging in the throes of death, but other than the nurses (who were wonderful, by the way) there was no one else around.

While sitting in the waiting area for hours I had occasion to talk to many, many mothers. Each one had a story that was so sad. Many of these preemie babies did not survive. Many of these parents had already gone through child loss, making this an even more nightmarish ordeal. Some of these little babies hung on tenaciously to life for six months or longer only to die of compli-cations. There was something desperately missing at this hospi-tal. Friends. These parents needed friends waiting with them. When a baby died, as was often the case, these parents were alone. Jonathan got to come home after just a few weeks. What about the others? What about the parents? I have often wondered how they coped all by themselves. I often think of that big, lonely hospital ward. I am left asking myself, "Where are the friends?" I am sure that every parent that faces the death of their little one alone in that intensive care unit is left wondering, "Where, oh where, are my friends?"

A casual friend of my husband's lost his little ten-year-old girl to complications from pneumonia last year. This young fa-ther was very reluctant to talk of this little girl's death with us, and it soon became quite evident why. Although he and his wife were at the hospital holding their daughter when she died, they needed something else to help them cope with this terrifying, lonely situation. They needed friends by their side. The man ex-plained that when death was imminent, he called a good friend of the family's to come to the hospital. He felt as though he and his wife were being swept away, and they needed to be anchored. Their friend did come and stayed by their side throughout their daughter's death. However, the reality of it all has now set in. They have three other children, but when one-fourth of you is taken away all at once, the pain can be unbearable. The grief hit their family hard. Much harder than they ever expected. Being a very religious family, many prayers were offered for this family. Cards were sent by the sack full. There was plenty of food brought to their home during those first few weeks after the death. And then there was that awful, intolerable, lonely silence. These parents were wounded clear through to their hearts, but the healing balm of friendship was absent.

Aloneness set in. Silent anguish became a part of their everyday living. The hurt that came through this young father's eyes was enough to pierce any heart. His stiffened face portrayed pain. His wife cannot — will not — speak of their daughter's death. Not yet. It is just too terribly painful. They are facing their first holidays without this little one who brought so much joy, so much activity into their home. This man looked at my husband and tearfully, painfully asked, "Where are my friends?"

I am often left wondering what would have happened to my own family when my 13-year-old sister died if we would have had the ongoing support, the very personal touch of friends nearby. Hindsight always provides so much wisdom and so many answers. Often it is far easier to understand things after time has elapsed. Answers often become much clearer to us as we look back over a period of time. Such is the case in the death of my sister Carmella.

My mother changed drastically after my sister's death, until her own eventual death, and I never understood why until many years later. She was left so totally alone, so completely alone, during her time of deepest need. My father left our home, so she did not have the comfort of a mate. She sank into a deep depression, and friends avoided her completely. Depressed people are certainly not much fun to be around. She let her physical self go, not combing her hair or bathing, which is so typical of deep grief and associated depression. She would stay in bed for days at a time. Her doctor, thinking he was helping, provided nerve pills to get her through this rough spell. Only the rough spell lasted for 24 years, each year getting a little bit worse, until her death. In looking back, I truly believe that grief took her heart away. She needed the touch of a friend to get her going again, but no one was there.

My mother learned so well the art of hiding her tears. It is

common, and is practiced by many people. This hiding of tears
and of our true feelings is used as a protective means of keeping
one from experiencing even deeper pain. Only, in the end, it does
not work because the pain is still there. I wonder what my mother's
life would have been like if one — only one — friend would
have hung in there with her through those tough hours of grief. I
am sure as she spent days at a time in bed without ever a friend
calling or coming by, she must have often wondered, *Where are
my friends? I thought I had so many, and now I can't even find
one.*

One day, about a year after my sister's death, my mother
was sitting in the old rocking char in our living room. She was
crying which was something she very rarely did. As kids we were
always taught to believe in God, to trust Him, and to call on Him
in prayer. Morning devotionals were not uncommon in my home.
So on this particular day I remember quite clearly reaching for
our large, black family Bible and handing it to my mother. "Here.
Read this. I know it will help." In my innocence, I did not know
what else to do to help ease her pain. She took that Bible and did
something which I will never forget. She threw it at me! "Get
that Bible away from me," she screamed. "That doesn't help.
Not one little bit!" I went off crying, not understanding at all
what she was talking about.

Today, I understand. At that moment in my mother's deep,
isolated grief over losing a daughter she loved with all of her
heart, those pages in the Bible seemed dead and empty. The life
was gone from those words written so neatly on the pages. She
needed someone to come to her, living those words of compassion and friendship. She needed someone to show her the love
that was found on those pages. She needed someone to dry her
tears. Someone to help her through those long, lonely nights of
remembering. Someone to help her get dressed and comb her
hair. She needed someone that never came. She needed a friend.

In my preparation for this book I had the privilege of talking with many, many families who suffered the agonizing pain
of child loss. One lady in particular stands out in my mind. She
is strikingly beautiful, and she spoke to me softly, almost with a
whisper. Hers was a story of shame. She never experienced child
loss personally, but the loss of her friend's child changed her
own life forever. She said that many years ago she and her best

friend each had one child, little boys, born to them around the same time. They both became pregnant again two years later, and they delivered beautiful little girls. They shared such fun times together, buying little pinafores and sunbonnets for the girls, and fishing poles and tackle boxes for the boys. They lived about a half hour's drive away from each other, so they tried to get together once a week, especially during the summer months.

One beautiful fall afternoon the families had a wonderful picnic together, then had a fun time playing baseball before calling it quits for the day. The next day, on a Sunday, this lovely lady received a panicked phone call from her friend. Her little son Bobby had become seriously ill during the night and was not expected to live through the day. He had been playing in the garage and had swallowed a mixture of lethal chemicals which had been mistakenly left out in the open. This beautiful lady with whom I was speaking became visibly shaken. She said, "Little Bobby died that evening at the age of four. I never went to the hospital, the funeral, or visited my best friend after that phone call. I just could not bring myself to face her." This lady went on to explain that she just felt like the two families had shared so many fun times together during the years that she just would not know how to act or what to say now that Bobby had died.

As the tears streamed down her face, I felt so sad. Best friends for years, and then when she was most needed, most wanted, she kept silent. She stayed away. Both families have grieved deeply over this for years I am sure.

I was somewhat stunned to hear this story, but then again, isn't that exactly what we have been talking about all along? Friends needing friends. Friends wanting to be friends, but not knowing how. Friends staying away during that crucial time of need during deep grief. Those grieving the loss of their child left asking the terrible question, *Where are my friends?*

At this point, when we are talking about the absolute necessity and the grave importance of friends, I feel a word needs to be said to those parents who find themselves suffering from another type of child loss not yet mentioned in this book. The loss of missing children. This, to me, would be the most excruciating of all losses because the finality of death can never come about until the child is found. And so many times the child is not ever found. Every day in this nation of ours we have the tragic abduction of children. Perhaps a child was walking home from school and never returned. Or maybe a child was riding his bike to a ball game. The bike is found but not the child. I used to worry every morning as my 12-year-old son Tim would leave the house at 5:30 a.m. to deliver the daily newspaper. I always breathed a sigh of relief as I would hear the door closing behind Tim when he returned home. Many, many parents have not been so fortunate. They have not heard the latch turn and the door open. A sickening feeling sets in, and the long, arduous search begins. A child is gone.

Two summers ago I was working outside in the garden with some of my children. It was almost dark and Stephanie, who was then four, decided to run through the field, across the yard to the house, to get a drink. She was thirsty, and she said she would wait for the rest of us at the house. "Don't spill the milk!" I yelled. "It's a full gallon, so be careful when you pour." About 15 minutes later the rest of us reached the house, and we found spilled milk all over the table, the chairs, and the floor. We started laughing. Poor Steph did it again! She was notorious for her spills.

All at once, we realized that Stephanie was missing. We started calling for her, but the house was silent — dead silent. "She must be hiding, ready to jump out and play a trick," one of the kids said. So, we began a search, each taking a bedroom, closet, or door to look behind. By now it was pitch dark outside and our home is surrounded by woods. Several acres of woods that would make it real easy to get lost, especially for a small four year old. A frightened one, at that. The five of us began to panic. What if Steph got scared and decided to run outside and was totally lost in the woods? By now, we were screaming for Stephanie to please answer us. We began circling the house, shining the flashlights into the woods. It was hopeless. An hour had passed. We were losing precious time. We could not find Stephanie. She was gone.

By now, my whole body was shaking uncontrollably. Flashes of John Walsh from television kept coming to my mind. I remember the nation's agony of waiting to find out where little Adam Walsh was after disappearing from a local shopping mall. He words stung my heart, as I pictured his tormented face on the television screen. "It's the not knowing that is so difficult. Please, if anyone can help us find Adam, I beg you to help."

"Stephanie," we kept screaming, "please answer us!" We decided to go through the house one more time quickly, then we were calling for outside help. As I stood screaming for Steph, looking at her empty bed, I thought I heard a small whimper. I screamed for all the other kids to come into the bedroom. Was I hallucinating, or did I hear a small voice. "Yes! Mom, we hear it, too!" Hiding underneath a pile of five blankets was Stephanie. She was sweaty, and her hair was soaked with tears. She was afraid that she would be in trouble for spilling the milk, so she hid herself away. As all of us gathered around Stephanie and hugged and kissed her literally hundreds of times my body continued to shake. What if? What if we had never found her? What if someone had been crouched by the house and had taken her? Our home has been broken into twice, so this was a real possibility.

For the first time in my life, I felt only a few moments of the sheer terror that parents must go through when the news arrives, "Your child is missing." Never, in all of my remaining days on this earth, do I ever want to feel that empty, that lost, that pained again. Not even for a few moments. Child loss of this nature is mind-boggling. It is totally inexplicable and unable to be fully comprehended unless you have personally gone through this sheer agony yourself. For those who have missing children, young men or women labeled as prisoners of war (POW's), those who are missing in action (MIA's), and you do not know the real whereabouts of your child, my heart literally breaks for you. Your pain in unable to be measured by human reasoning. I can only pray that somehow God enters your life and gives you a measure of peace, wisdom, and calm unknown to all others about you.

Parents who suffer child loss of this cruel nature need friends. Not just for a day, or a week, or a month. They need friends forever, because their grief is never ending. There can be no final chapter as long as the child is still missing. In our daily hustle and routine of living, our minds get caught up in such meaningless trivialities. The parents of missing children have one thing on their minds constantly: their missing child. That child is always in the forefront of their thoughts. The grief continues hour after hour, day after day, year after year. Friends who continue to remember are needed so desperately. These parents need to hear an occasional word of hope, and they need to hear many words of comfort and love. Death is not an option in this type of child loss; it is not a door that can be closed. Friends, caring friends, are needed, not for just six months or a year, but for a lifetime.

When I see pictures of missing children on milk cartons, hanging in the post office, or in the local department store, the reality of this type of child loss sets in. There are, right at this moment, children missing. Precious children missing, never to be found again. It is difficult to even think about this, yet the rows and rows of pictures of these children make this child loss seem all too real. The parents of these children need help. They need to be remembered. They need the constant, continuous touch of friends. They need daily reminders that someone cares. And so often, far too often, we get busy in our own living and we forget the continuous, nagging pain of those who suffer from missing children. My Stephanie was only missing for a little more than an hour and I thought I was ready to lose my mind. I cannot in my wildest imagination begin to understand the sheer terror and pain that parents must go through when they actually find out that their child is truly missing. Gone. Never to be found again. Many of these parents are left asking the heartbreaking question, *Where, oh where, are my friends?*

When the reality of the loss of a child sets in, this settling-in period of truly understanding that your child is gone is often the most painful of all times to go through. Nothing at all seems right. Nothing looks right. Nothing feels right. Even the shining sun doesn't look so bright or feel so warm upon your face. Everything is turned topsy-turvy. In many ways, a person that has lost a child has experienced a portion of personal death. This particular period of hurting can be devastating to the marriage relationship.

When both a mother and father are suffering from aching hearts, they need someone to help them get through the simple tasks of the day. When parents are left alone in their grief asking the question, *Where are my friends?* it is crucial for them to pull together. Often, they do not. This period of grief is often a time of feeling alone and abandoned by everyone, including even your mate. Instead of holding onto each other in grief, many couples do exactly what their friends do. They avoid the topic of their child's death. The loss is real. They know it. The pain is real.

They feel it. But the words to comfort just will not come. It is simply too painful.

When we risk baring our souls in grief, we are in essence saying, "I am hurting, and I need your help." For many husbands and wives this baring of the souls becomes almost impossible because anger, guilt, and blame follow so closely behind grief. It is so easy when in intense mental pain, to shout out in blame and anger things that we would ordinarily never, ever say. Unfortunately, this is what is done between a husband and wife so much of the time during this period of deep hurting. Something terribly bad, terribly wrong, has happened, and in our reasoning someone should bear the blame. "If only you had kept the house picked up and not left the button on the floor, our baby would not have choked to death." "If only you had not taken that aerobics class the umbilical cord would not have strangled the baby." "If only you would have watched her at the pool, she would not have drowned." "If only you had insisted on him wearing his seat belt, he would still be alive." "If only you had not left the paint thinner out, he would not have gotten into the poison." On and on the blame goes. We need someone to lash out to in our painful anger and anguish. However, when we pierce our grieving mate, the pain we inflict, the words we say will never be totally forgotten. How can they be? Once this bond of friendship and intimate love between a husband and a wife begins to crumble it is difficult, and often impossible, to restore the relationship fully. Husbands and wives need to hold each other up, not tear each other down. Especially during this painful period of child loss. They need to be each other's friend. Others have vanished from the scene. The last thing on earth that parents need to feel at this time is abandonment from each other.

It is still very difficult at times for my husband and me to talk freely and openly about our losses. If I mention something especially painful, I see the grieved look on my husband's face, and I know that he is having a particularly hurtful day. I know that I need to draw him close. Often words are not shared; only a hand is held. That is enough to say, "I love you, and I am hurting with you." If I am in a particularly bad mood, my husband is often able to recognize that I am hurting over the loss of one of our children. There has been some painful reminder. He will know to pull me close to him, brush the hair from my face, and wipe away the tears. Most often, words are not shared between us during these hurting moments. A simple touch, an arm around the waist, a kiss on the cheek are the reinforcements needed. Those few moments together, holding onto each other, seem to give the encouragement and the strength needed to go on.

It takes real effort to do this, though. Child loss is never, ever easy to deal with. It is much easier to pull away, remain silent, or to yell out in anger something that really hurts. There have been many times when my husband has chosen to walk out the door and go to work, leaving me crying. He just cannot deal with the tears right at the moment. That is really hurtful to me, and the tears just seem to flow all the more. What I wanted, what I needed, were a few words saying how much he cares, a tender touch, and a strong arm to hold me for a few seconds. For him, it was much easier to walk away. When he comes home in the evening, if I am still crying or just plain not being myself, he will often excuse himself to go to his office. I know that this is his way of escaping the reality of the pain that is still there. It is easier for him to go into a room, close the door, and forget about things for a while. That is often how a man will deal with pain. When I am hurting and crying all that I need is for my husband to be there, to hold me for a while, and to talk with me. His walking away really adds to the pain that I am already feeling. Women seem to want to talk, to need to talk, about their pain. These are real differences in grieving that need to be dealt with within the marriage. And it is just plain difficult to do. It's much easier to just walk away until things seems to lighten up a bit. The only problem is that walking away never eases the pain.

When a husband hurts over losing a child, sometimes it is unbearable to share that pain with his wife. Husbands are supposed to be strong, protective, and keep the family going. At least, that is what society teaches us. Somehow men are not supposed to show their true feelings of pain. What a burden society has placed on fathers who have lost children! Thank goodness this idea is slowly beginning to change. Men hurt so badly and are afraid to show it. When a man feels weak, he feels useless. These feelings are certainly never good for any marriage. This thinking carries over into the marriage, unfortunately. Many times a man's grief turns into silence and a total withdrawal, or bitter anger towards his wife. The grief of child loss within the marriage is then greatly magnified.

A woman is allowed to cry by society's rules. Only not too much. If she becomes too emotional she is often labeled as being on the very verge of a mental breakdown. So she, in her feelings of abandonment, often tries to subdue the tears, and instead her pain comes out in a raging anger. Remember my mother with the Bible? A woman will especially lash out at her husband. After all, he is supposed to be the stronger one. A wife is many times left asking two questions: *Where are my friends?* And, *Where in the world is my husband?*

May I urge every grieving couple to grieve the loss of your child together? You are both in agony. You both may feel rejected by your mutual friends. You both feel somewhat abandoned by those closest to you. You both lost a part of the "unified you." No one else in this entire world will feel the same intensity of pain as you both will feel together as a couple. Child loss is such a unique loss. In your anguish, do not push away from each other. Rather, cry together. Share your thoughts and feelings together. Hurt together. When evening falls and the house is so quiet that you can actually feel the death of your child, hold onto each other. When the night is so lonely that you think you will die, pull close to one another. When you each need a friend, be that friend for one another.

Friends will undoubtedly disappoint you. Life goes on for others despite our intense personal grief. This is a difficult, yet true, fact to face. Very rare is a friend who will hang in there with you when you are despondent, lonely, angry, and depressed. We all love to be near people that lift our spirits, not people who pull us down. Child loss is an unpleasant, uncomfortable, unnatural thing to deal with. So most people, over the long haul, will avoid the topic at all costs. That is why it is so very crucial for parents to hurt together. Be patient with one another. Be wise enough to know that you need each other now more than ever before. Be that friend for each other that you both so desperately need. It is okay to cry. It is okay to feel so alone that you want to die. It is okay to feel deserted by the entire world. But, it's not okay to do it alone. Hold on to each other more now than at any other time. You share such a personal loss — your child. You need to help each other.

Where are my friends? Eventually, probably they are getting on with their own lives. *Where is my mate?* Hopefully, by your side.

When you are looking for a friend, remember that sometimes, many times, friends are hard to come by. Friends hurt for you, too. They also grieve over your loss. They often feel like total failures because of their inability to help. No one's heart hurts like yours, however. You cannot expect anyone to feel the depth of pain that you do. It is just not humanly possible. Do not be afraid to call on your friends in your times of need. Usually they will respond. Allow them to learn to grieve with you. Do not be afraid to shed your tears with a friend. True friends will help wipe away your tears, and not criticize you because of them. I wish that my own mother had understood that she could have called on a friend to help. Instead, she withdrew. She did what was easiest to do. Remember how in her deepest, loneliest despair she did not want anything to do with the family Bible? She had not lashed her anger at God. Her anger was aimed at all of those who professed to be her friends, but who abandoned her in her deepest time of need. She needed someone to take her hand and pray with her, not pray from a far away distance for her. She needed a friend to help her draw nearer to God. She needed a bit of help to lead her through those dark days into the comforting arms of Jesus. She needed someone to show her that God was real.

Above all we need to always remember that there is one faithful Friend who remains by our side at all times. When our friends leave, when our mate leaves, this Friend is still there. Always there. He never, ever leaves. He always cares. He deeply cares. He offers peace and calm. He understands our questions and our moods. He forgives our angry, hurtful words. He understands our pain. God is a true friend that is always near. Hold fast to God when you think that your heart is literally going to break in two. When no one will listen, talk to Him through prayer. It helps so very much. When you feel like crying, don't hide your tears. Allow your tears to flow freely. He will comfort you. Allow Him to help you. He will. You can be fully assured of that blessed promise that He will never leave you or forsake you. Especially not when you have lost a child. "Where are your friends?" Your best Friend has never left. He is standing right by your side.

Chapter 4

"Nobody Cares"

Have you ever been through some kind of deep hurt or loss, and you are left feeling like absolutely nobody cares? Most all of us experience this feeling from time to time. We lose our job. Nobody cares. We cannot get our mortgage money approved to buy our home. Nobody cares. We have to drop out of college due to lack of finances. Nobody cares. We are overworked and underpaid. Nobody cares. We are trying so hard to live a good, godly life and everything seems to go all wrong. Nobody cares. Our good health is suddenly taken away. Nobody cares. Our child dies. Nobody cares.

All of the losses that have been mentioned have some sort of remedy, some sort of hope — except the loss of a child. That loss is final. That is a fact we must one day learn to live with. That loss is a reality we must face. Our child is gone forever. There simply is not hope of changing that one certainty. And so very often it seems like nobody even cares.

As the months pass after the loss of a child, life for others has gone back to a normal routine. Rushing to and fro. Busy at work. Making vacation plans. Going to the movies. Planning for the holidays. For a parent who is suffering from child loss, the entire world takes on a new look. Things that once seemed so urgent, so important, no longer seem to have much significance at all. Child loss changes our priorities real fast. What once seemed to have a life urgency no longer even seems worth mentioning. It just does not seem to be that terribly important if our bathroom towels are frayed and do not match. Who really cares? What we miss are the giggles of the child that once so happily played in a bubble bath in that tub. It just does not seem life threatening if the kitchen floor gets waxed once a week. What is important is that we miss the little feet that once tracked up that kitchen floor. And nobody seems to understand, much less care. We are left wondering if anyone even remembers our child.

When early child loss occurs, such as with miscarriage, still-born, or premature birth resulting in death, often it does seem like nobody cares from the very onset of the loss. People usually do one of two things. They either totally ignore the topic that you lost a child or they say things that really do more harm than good. We have already talked about why people tend to like the silent avenue of dealing with things such as child loss. It is just a whole lot easier. Inappropriate words will be talked about more in length in another chapter. I have not figured out which I think is worse — the silence or the wrong words. Both hurt and both leave you, the hurting parent, feeling like there is nobody that really cares.

Silence definitely sends a loud message, and that message is that nobody cares. Silence shouts to us in our pain. While it is most definitely not always true that silence means that nobody cares, it does give you the feeling that that's how it is. When our little boy was stillborn, I used to pray for the phone to ring, hop-ing that somebody, anybody, would call to ask how we were do-ing. I used to wait for the mail to arrive, hoping that someone would send a card just saying that we were remembered. I re-ceived a total of four cards which I have saved in a special place. I still pull out these cards from time to time to remind me that some people really did care. There were some phone calls for a while from my sister and my husband's parents; then the phone, too, was silent. There seemed to be no big upset in anyone's life when we lost that little boy, except in our lives. Our lives were totally ripped apart for a while. We had never been so sad in all of our lives. We needed, wanted, some help and support. I real-ize now how uncomfortable other people were to even hear about this little boy. It is now eight years since his death, and people still will not talk to me about it. Every time I bring up the topic, even in a small way, people look the other way, get a strange look on their faces, and then there is silence. For a long, long time it felt as though nobody cared. I now understand that they did care; they just did not know to express their caring.

Several weeks after the death of the child is the time when the reality of it all begins to settle in. This is the time when the parents have cried and cried until they feel that another tear cannot possibly fall from their swollen eyes. It hurts so badly that nothing in the entire world seems like it will ever feel happy again. It feels as though a dark curtain has been pulled down over your eyes, and everything that is seen is tainted and clouded. Lives have been turned inside out and upside-down. Plans for the future have been thwarted. Reminders of the child are everywhere. There is no desire to even move from a chair, let alone get up and get back to work.

But life continues on for others, and somehow, some way, parents who have lost children are expected to get up and go on, too. Most work places only give three days off from work for a death. I find this terribly difficult to understand.

Early child loss is probably the easiest to be dismissed by others, especially in the case of miscarriage, or second and third trimester pregnancy loss. No one shared the expected joy of your little one quite like you and your husband. Most couples share extremely intimate talks during pregnancy, sharing their hopes and desires for this new life that is so longed for, so anticipated. When that young life ends abruptly, all of those dreams and hopes for the future end abruptly, too. Parents must shift gears immediately. Words cannot adequately explain what this is like. For weeks you may have been talking about this precious little bundle, and now all at once this little bundle of joy is gone. Forever. Who can possibly understand your disappointment? Who can ever begin to understand the sadness that now fills the place where there was once so much joy? Plans for the nursery are stopped. Gazing into the store windows at little newborn clothes brings only tears. Even the smell of baby powder or baby lotion can cause a parent to burst into tears. Unfortunately, most people around us do not even begin to understand any of this. The baby was not real at all to them. They see this abrupt loss as nothing major because this little one never shared your home or your lives. You cannot miss what you never had. How very wrong!

A baby becomes a very real, very joyous part of your life from the moment you learn of conception. That child was a physical part of his mother, a very real part of her. And that child also had a daddy. Very, very few people understand what a deep bond of love can be formed very early in a pregnancy. And when this little life is gone, so much joy is gone, too. The world about you seems to go on as though nothing happened. There may be a momentary pause to say, "I'm sorry," but most often it seems as though nobody really cares about your deep, personal hurt. The baby clothes are quietly packed away in a box, along with your expectations for this child. A silent type of grief begins to set in. Why try to talk about something that so few understand? Why share our hurts when others just look at us in silence? Truly it seems that nobody cares.

Several months ago I received a phone call from a friend expressing a need to talk. About a year ago she lost a baby to an unexpected first trimester miscarriage. She had just told all of her friends and family members of her wonderful news. Now, she had to tell them of her loss, and it really hurt. She had a difficult time conceiving this child, and that made matters even worse. The pain really came through in her conversation. She and her husband wanted this baby so very, very much.

I talked to her initially when I heard of her loss. Since I had gone through several miscarriages, I explained to her some of the feelings she and her husband would probably go through. She said that talk really helped. She had been feeling guilty for not being truly happy for others who so cheerfully announced their pregnancies. She said that now, after a year had passed, it seemed like everyone was oblivious to her loss. Even her own parents didn't seem to understand what she was going through. Her brother and his wife just announced a pregnancy, and she said that their new baby is the topic of discussion at every family gathering. Everyone is so happy for her brother — everyone except her. She is happy, but not totally. She wishes that she was pregnant, too. She said, "I could be a whole lot happier if only they said they were still hurting for me. Even just a little bit. It just seems like nobody cares anymore."

When child loss occurs later on, after a child has been a viable, active part of a family, people at least make a conscientious effort for a while to share in your sorrow. Time is supposed to heal; it does not always work that way in child loss, though. Most experts agree that real grief does not even begin until at least six months following the death of a child. Up until that time most parents are in somewhat of a clouded stupor, not really understanding at all the depth or the finality of death and separation. During this period of time it is not unusual for parents to continue to set the table for the child that has died, to prepare their child's favorite foods, to think that they saw their child in a shopping mall. Quite often parents will walk through the door expecting the child to be home waiting for them.

Unfortunately, while these frightening changes and new adjustments are occurring with the parents who have lost their child, friends are now back to their usual routine of living. They are busy at work, performing civic volunteer duties, rushing to and fro, and somehow the hurting parents have been left to grieve alone. At least that is the way it all seems.

I read a lengthy newspaper article about a mother who lost her 16-year-old son last winter in a school bus accident. She tells of the initial shock of sitting in her office, hearing of the accident. She then relates the details following the next six months after her son's death. She went back to work, hoping to find support and concern following the death of her son Chris. But she found herself crying alone a lot of the time, with most people staring at her silently or whispering about her odd behavior in a corner of the office. Somehow, they figured that she should be over her grief by now. After all, six months had passed!

She continues the story by relating that she finally broke down and talked to a close friend. She told her friend that what she really wanted, what she really needed, was to hear her son's name mentioned. He was Chris. They all knew him. He had visited the office quite frequently. The office employees all knew Chris. But, no one said a word. They acted as though nobody cared that Chris was gone. Chris was real. Chris was a terrific kid. Chris was her son! And no one even mentioned his name after his death. To this mother, the message was clear: nobody cared.

I found my eyes dripping tears as I read of this mother's account of feeling so alone. So many people go through this same type of pain. We all seem so afraid to mention the child's name. Parents are well aware that they had a child that died. They want to hear their child's name. They want you to remember their child. When a child dies, it is so very important for parents to be able to talk freely about their child.

When my husband and I moved to Oklahoma City in 1970 to continue our education we had the good fortune of meeting someone at church who has remained one of our dearest friends on this earth — Doug Lawyer. My husband had the very special opportunity of working as a youth minister side by side with Doug who served as the pulpit minister for a large church in Oklahoma City. In less than a week we knew more about Doug than most people learn about others in a lifetime. Doug likes to talk. In his talking Doug told us of the tragic loss of his little son Dougie to leukemia. Little Doug's death was briefly mentioned in a previous chapter of this book. Doug and his wife, Charla, suffered a tremendous loss when their little Dougie died. It was not an easy death. It was slow and painful. And the loss of that special little boy still causes great pain today.

When making preparations for this book I called on Doug for some help. I asked him if he ever went through a lonely spell after Dougie died when he felt that nobody cared. Doug's answer was so truly typical of Doug. "No. Never. I knew that people cared. They didn't always know how to express it, but I knew that they cared. They had to. I talked about my precious Dougie boy all of the time. I still do."

Doug chose a path that most people who are grieving do not always take. He refused to be silent about his son's death. That little boy was special. He was so precious. He was a God-given gift, and Doug intended to tell the entire world about him. Even if hearing about his son's death made people uncomfortable. Even if they didn't want to listen. Even if it seemed like nobody cared. Doug made sure people knew of his grief, and by so doing did not allow his personal grief to swallow him up into a shell of silence. Doug is one of only a few that I know of who can do this type of thing, though. It is much, much easier to be held tightly by the grip of silence, than to stir people's feelings of discomfort.

Parents need help while hurting from child loss. They need special, caring people as their friends. People who will not expect them to be healed of all hurt six months down the road. That is when the intense grief is just beginning. The first birthday. The first Christmas. The first Thanksgiving. The first vacation. The first family reunion. Each one of these firsts is devastating.

They all mark a first without that special child. To have people that do not even mention your child's name makes the grief bitterly unbearable. One is left feeling like nobody — absolutely nobody cares.

My sister died on June 6, 1965, at the age of 13. The first major family holiday we faced without her was Thanksgiving. Since my father had already left home, my family now consisted of my mother, myself (16), and my little sister (7). My grandmother always hosted the traditional Thanksgiving dinner at her small house in the country. This would be our first year to spend Thanksgiving day home alone. My mother just did not feel like going anywhere. The loneliness had really hit hard. So the three of us ate cold sandwiches at our little kitchen table in a quiet, lonely house. Remembering. And as we remembered, the silence grew so very loud. The phone never rang. No one came to our door to see how we were. We couldn't wait for the day to end. It just seemed that nobody, absolutely nobody, even cared.

The first Christmas without my sister was just as awful. My mother refused to shop for any gifts or to put up a Christmas tree. By now she was sinking into a deep depression. She wanted no Christmas celebration at all. At the time I did not understand. Today, I certainly do. My mother was hurting so badly. What joy could she possibly have when so much had been taken away? I, on the other hand, wanted some sort of normalcy to come back into our home. I shopped for my little sister, bought a live tree which we would later plant in memory of my sister who had died, and wrapped gifts alone on Christmas Eve. My mother stayed in bed all Christmas Day, while I tried to put together a toy oven with all of those crazy directions that I still cannot read even today. There was no Christmas dinner that day, no home-baked cookies, no festivity. My mother was buried deep in grief, and our home remained very sadly silent.

The next first we had to face was my sister's birthday, January 23. This, of course, was only a few weeks following Christmas. It was just one year before that she had been taken off to the Bacharach Home for the terminally ill. All of these "firsts" to go through. My mother was alone and deeply depressed. My father was alone and suffering. Two other children didn't know what was really happening. And silence. That awful silence. No one came by to visit. No one sent a card of remembrance. No one even asked if we were okay. It truly seemed that nobody cared.

I still have my moments of wondering even today if people truly did not care, of if they just did not know what to do to help. Or did they possibly think that after a year it was time to move on and get back among the living? Probably it was a combination of all three. We tend to put such limitations on people, and want to enforce guidelines for people to live by. Even in the area of child loss. Especially in the area of grief.

My husband had an occasion a few months back to meet with an older couple who lost all five of their children. This, to me, is totally beyond the realm of comprehension. The story was tragic as each incident of a child's death unfolded. A stillbirth. A terminally ill child. A car accident claimed another life. Complications from surgery claimed another. And one more car accident. How in the world did they cope?

The wife is the one who told the story, stopping occasionally to cry. She showed my husband pictures of each one of her five children. So proud of each one. The husband sat quietly in the corner of a room, wiping his eyes from time to time with a handkerchief. He finally quietly got up and excused himself. I am sure that the pain was just too much to bear. It must have hurt so terribly to recount each tragic death of a child.

As I listened to this almost unbelievable story of loss, my heart literally hurt. Losing one child leaves such a void, such an emptiness. But, to have every child taken. That is almost more than I can bear to hear about. I could not help but wonder if their friends still remember them. I pray that this couple has never had to say, "It just seems so much like nobody cares."

When I delivered a stillborn son, a dear friend, Alice Ryan, who was the head of the obstetrical ward at the hospital at the time, helped with the delivery. Alice has always been special to me and my family. On more than one occasion she allowed me to "sneak" kids up to the window of my hospital room to take a peek at their new baby brother or sister. She pretended not to see, when I knew full well that she knew what was going on. She shared in some of my happiest moments; now she would share in one of my most sad moments. I remember after my husband left to go home that evening, Alice came to briefly talk with me. Her words would later help me many times over. She said, "You have just gone through a very painful experience. But, your pain has just begun. There will be many times when it seem like nobody cares — not even your husband." On hearing those words, I did not know what Alice meant. Later on, I would replay those words over and over again.

We have already talked some about the differences between a man's grief and a woman's grief. Let me reiterate that a woman gets hit twice. She not only has the emotional loss to deal with but the physical loss, too. Carrying a baby inside of your body is special, to say the least. It is an incredible feeling. That first fluttery kick will always be remembered by a mother. I always loved being pregnant. It never seemed like a burden, but rather a special privilege. To actually feel life inside of your body is indescribable. Giving birth is a totally fascinating, miraculous event. I never once found the pain of childbirth to be unbearable because the joy of birth was so overwhelmingly wonderful. The physical bond between a mother and child cannot adequately be put into words. It is something that must be felt in order to be understood.

When a child dies, not just the emotional bond of love is affected, but a very physical part of a mother dies, too. And a woman can try all she wants to explain this to a man, but he will not ever fully understand. He *cannot* fully understand. It was not his body that changed, stretched, grew, adapted, and performed amazing feats to nurture a life. I am crying as I am writing this, because my mind and body still have not fully adjusted to my losses. And I know that I never will completely feel whole again. How can I? Part of "me" is gone. A vital part of me is gone. I lost that part of me each time I lost a child. Alice was so right. At times it seems like nobody cares. Not even my husband. His body does not remind him every month of child loss. Mine does. And it really, really hurts. It is an emptiness that just will not go away. Nothing fills the void. Ever. And nobody seems to care. Not the way you do.

As I am writing this particular portion of this book, it is nearing Christmas time. I am sitting in a quiet room very late at night with my youngest daughter, Alex, sleeping by my side. I pause to look at the tree with all of the lights, and I listen to the wind howling outside. It was a bitter cold day today, and a fresh snow has fallen. We celebrated our son Chris's 18th birthday yesterday, and he will be leaving for college in three weeks to join three other brothers in Arkansas. I am filled with such mixed emotions. Happy to see my children growing, but sad to see them leaving home.

A few days ago I took our 14-year-old daughter to the doctor to try to track down the reason for her chest pains. Possible mitral valve. There will be tests completed this week. As I watched Cherie baking cookies today, my mind wondered. What if? Just what if all does not turn out well? How would I live life without her? When I enter the hospital with her this week for tests, I will be reminded of that very possibility. I find myself looking again at little Alex sleeping by me, and then I stare at that lopsided Christmas tree. I am reminded of just how fragile and fleeting life really is. I am reminded of how much I miss my boys when they are away at college. I can still write to them and talk to them on the phone. But I miss them! I miss their very presence. I wonder what that tree would look like next year if one of my children was really missing. Forever missing. I shudder at the thought. And I spend some time crying. Silly, to some. But not to me.

I know two families dealing with terminally ill children right now. This is, in all likelihood, their last Christmas together. What must that be like? To know that separation is inevitable. I write to them often and try to share in their pain. But ultimately, when the final moment of death arrives, I know that they, too, will say that it feels like nobody cares. Because nobody, absolutely nobody, cares like a parent. The loss of a child is so personal. So intimate. So unique. Even when people honestly try to feel your pain, it still seems like nobody cares. The pain is just that deep and hurts that badly. And losing a child literally takes a heart and breaks it in two.

How do husbands and wives stay unified during this critical period when all of life seems to go back to normal except for them? Their entire household has been changed by the loss of a child. Meals are different. Watching television is different. Picnics are different. Going to the store is different. Every single area of life has been affected by the loss of a child. As I am writing my stomach feels achy and a bit sick as I think about these things. One child brings so much activity, conversation, noise, laughter, amusement, and life into a home. When that child is gone, home does not seem like home any more. Not now. Not for a long, long time. Yet our society, in its rushed thinking, tells us to move on. Get busy. Fill up our time with other things. Forget. Look ahead.

I heard an amazing story of a young man killed in an automobile accident recently. His family never shed one tear when he died. The father preached the funeral. The five remaining brothers and sisters sat upright throughout the funeral service. The mother said that God gave this child to them for a brief while, and now he has been taken away. They all said, "This is God's will." A friend of mine who attended the service thought this was so great. I find the entire scene to be totally unreal and unnatural. Yes. I believe in God. Yes. I believe I have a strong faith and an unwavering allegiance to my God. But I can also assure you that it would not be life as usual if my son was killed in an automobile accident. My husband and I, along with the rest of the children, would have a long pause in our normal routine of living. In fact, nothing would be normal for a long, long time. I would not be ashamed. I would cry lots. My husband would grieve openly. And life would be very difficult to live. Forever changed. How do I know? Because just the mere thought, the faint possibility of such a loss causes me to hurt from the inside out.

How do I think my friends would react to my loss? I can say with almost certainty that almost everyone would expect things to be back to normal in a very short period of time. We are trained to think this way. We are somehow led to believe that something is very, very wrong with us if we do not cope, and cope well, almost immediately. We live in such a rushed, hushed society. Even our grieving is rushed and hushed. No wonder we are left feeling isolated, abandoned, alone, and wondering if anybody really, truly cares.

Husbands have a real burden placed on them to be strong. Always. No matter what. It seems as though everything from society to religion says that men must be strong. I think our society is particularly guilty of imposing this misconception on men. In talking with my family doctor, Dr. Hay, we discussed this at some length. He said that he was always taught that men were to stay somewhat detached from death. As a doctor he had to be around death a great deal, so detachment became part of his life. It had to. He really thought he could handle death well. Until . . . the death of his father. And the emotions were there. The feelings of extreme pain and loss over someone dearly loved. This stage of loss where nobody seems to care is probably the most critical stage for a marriage. If we are left feeling that even our spouse does not care, then we have nothing, no one left to hold on to.

Because husbands grieve differently than women, and so much is expected of men so soon, they often appear to be non-caring. Many men gave a great deal of difficulty with verbalizing their feelings to begin with. How in the world can they now be expected to verbalize their deep grief over losing a child? Men, fathers, seem to have so much stacked against them in this area of grief. Men are, by nature, great leaners. By that I mean that they very often prefer to lean on their wives for moral and emotional support. Most times this turns out to be okay, except in the case of child loss. A wife does not want a leaner for a husband. Not at this time in her life. She is looking for a support, someone *she* can lean on. It is here that we have a major problem. A husband looks to his wife to comfort him, console him, talk to him, cradle him, and be physically intimate with him during this lonely period of child loss. After all, if nobody else cares, he needs to know that his wife cares.

A wife, on the other hand, is suffering physical and emotional pain from child loss. She needs so desperately to be held close, to be talked to, to have a shoulder to put her head on. She needs to be told over and over that things will one day get better. She may not desire physical intimacy at this point in her grief. Part of her body feels like it is missing, like it has been violated. She needs no more violation at this critical point. This is often a terribly difficult concept for a man to understand.

It takes a lot of patience and commitment to get through this period. The male and female, husband and wife, needs are so critically different. Most couples do not even begin to understand these differences. If these very basic differences are not taken into consideration, marital problems may become difficult to resolve. When a husband and wife are already feeling quite abandoned by their friends, it is most important for them to draw close to each other, to listen to one another, and to be a friend. But, sadly, far too often, there is a cold silence that begins between the husband and wife.

When a silence sets in, this is where so many problems

between husbands and wives begin. There already may be feelings of guilt and anger over the loss of this child. Now there are deep feelings of abandonment. If not dealt with properly a couple may not survive the rigors that they face, especially if left alone without the constant help and support of close friends.

Please, please remember that you both dearly loved this child. Your lives, both separately and together, have been drastically changed and affected by your child's death. Men and women handle grief differently. This is a fact that you both must take into consideration. Men may work longer hours, trying to avoid home and its painful reminders. They may take up drinking, and even become somewhat harsh and distant toward their wife. They are looking for some physical closeness and affection. Grieving men actually need a strong, supportive woman at this point.

A wife handles things quite differently. She tends to cry her heart out. Her emotions are going crazy. She feels actual physical pain from child loss. Her arms ache. Her back hurts. She may have severe headaches. If early child loss has occurred, she may imagine she is still pregnant. She needs to talk. She wants to stay home among the many reminders. She needs to feel that the child was real. She wants strong arms to hold her, and someone to tenderly wipe away her tears. She wants a husband to make it all better.

Can you begin to see the problems that child loss brings, especially for grieving couples? When grief sets in so deeply, and it seems like nobody cares, it is crucial for a husband and wife to cry together, talk together, to share their feelings together. It takes a real concerted effort from both to draw close to one another. If a grief bond is not formed at this time, you are setting yourself up for even more grief.

One man who lost a young son due to an accident that happened at home blamed his wife for being negligent. She was not properly watching their little boy, he thought. The little boy played with cleaning chemicals, ingested some, and ultimately died. A tragic, accidental poisoning.. The mother of this little boy was overburdened with guilt. You can well imagine how horrible she felt. She loved this little boy so very much, and now he was gone. The father refused to forgive. He became very angry and bitter. Their marriage began to fall apart. Finally, as a last resort, they decided to get some much needed grief counseling. The father very hesitantly attended a few sessions. The mother willingly went, and little by little she began to get some support. What had happened was a horrendous accident. But, it was still an accident. She needed so much the love and forgiveness of her husband. Unfortunately, that never happened. His anger turned into bitter hatred, not just for his wife, but for life in general. It is now ten years after the death of this little boy. The mother and father divorced. And the father is a slave to alcoholism. He never got beyond the "nobody cares" stage. In his eyes, he had been handed a bad deal, and nobody, including his wife, ever cared.

It was related to me that this man, this hurt father, showed up at a meeting for the bereaved less than a year ago. He had been drinking, and looked a mess. He shouted some angry words at the instructor who happens to be a friend of mine. Then, he said the saddest words on the face of this earth. "Nobody cared. Not a person in the whole world ever cared." As he left the instructor was stunned, as were the other people. But, she said, "You know, he was so right. Nobody did care. Not enough, anyway. Even when he burst through the doors of this meeting, not one of us got up to hold him, to allow him to cry. Instead, we watched him shout out in his pain."

I don't know when a story has ever touched me more. It is so much easier to tell people just how the ABC's of grief should be than it is to give them a shoulder to lean on. This man and his wife desperately needed friends who cared and they needed each other. They found neither, and their lives were ruined.

This "nobody cares" stage seems to be almost too much to handle. Friends that say it is time to get back up on your feet and start living again do not understand what you are going through. Grief from losing your child has just begun to settle in. And there are always problems that come about with your spouse. Both are deep in grief, but each grieving so differently that it seems even your spouse doesn't care. Nobody cares. Absolutely nobody in the whole world cares that your child is gone.

Almost every parent alive who has lost a child goes through a period of aloneness — total isolation. A time of feeling abandoned and rejected. A feeling that nobody cares. And that parent is so very correct in his thinking. Nobody does care — not to the degree that you, the parent, does. My child losses are unique to me, and me alone. Even my husband does not share all of the same grief and pain that I do. We each hurt. Our friends hurt for us. But not with the intensity that I hurt. At some point I had to realize that this is a fact. Nobody does care. Not quite like I do. I cannot expect them to. If I turn my pain into angry bitterness then I end up losing even more. This period of feeling that nobody cares is probably the most difficult period to get through in child loss. It is so difficult, mostly because it is true.

Many couples seek the help of support groups such as Compassionate Friends at this point. You can talk with other parents who have gone through these feelings, and are now able to move on. In my talking with parents I found that this decision is extremely personal. Help groups comforted some simply by allowing them to share their pain. Others said it was too depressing to sit around and hear each other's sad stories of loss. My advice would be to do what your heart leads you to do. Only you can know what will help you. Above all else, make a positive attempt to do something. Do not allow yourself to become enveloped in a silent vacuum of grief. Your feelings may one day harden your already-broken heart.

As I talked with Dr. Hay, my family physician, about the problem of nobody caring, he explained something to me. Something that I already knew, but needed to hear again. "Like it or not, life goes on despite our loss. We must learn that life is for the living, or we will never get beyond our grief." At first I was a bit angry with Dr. Hay for saying this. I even expressed my feelings to my husband that day after speaking with Dr. Hay. About two weeks later his wise words began to sink in. He was so right. We can remain angry and upset at the entire world because our child died, and it seems like nobody cares. But, in spite of our anger, our pain, and our hurt, life continues on. That is just how it is. We can feel cheated. We can hate our spouse. We can place blame on others. But that still does not bring back our child. Nothing will change that one sad, lonely fact.

I am crying right now as I am writing this. How I wish those words were not true. I wish that every parent that has lost a child could have just one chance, one little hope, of changing that awful fact. But it cannot happen. It just will not happen. And while it is true that nobody will care as deeply as we do, we must not let our tears turn us bitter. We need to remember the wisdom found in Dr. Hay's words. "Life is for the living." It is a lonely, difficult trek from the depths of despair to the light of the living, but the climb begins one faltering step at a time.

I urge you to love your friends in spite of it seeming like they do not care. Most friends do care. They just do not know what to do or say to show you that they truly do care. And when your heart is breaking into pieces, know that your mate's heart is breaking into pieces, too. Reach out to each other. Keep trying. Hold on to each other through this storm of lonely despair. Your child is gone. Naturally you feel weakened and alone. Just grab hold of a hand and hold on. Begin that slow, painful walk back to life together. The road is rough and rocky. The hill back to life is steep. You will need help. So hold on to each other. Forgive. Try to understand. Hurt together. Dry each other's tears. You cannot expect others to share your intimate, private pain as deeply as you do. This child you lost was yours. Only the two of you can share the depth of pain that you now feel. Pull towards one another. Your walk back to life will become stronger.

And finally, remember that there is a Friend who does share our sorrow, who does truly care. God is by our side and is there to help. David, the shepherd, cried out to God many times over in the Psalms for help. He felt so abandoned and so alone. But he found that God was always right where He said He would be — by David's side. Job, in his anguish, felt abandoned by his friends. Even his wife offered him no encouragement. In his anguish he cried out to God. And God gently but firmly reminded Job to look at all the majesty, all the life around him. God had not left his side. God was still right there.

When you feel as though absolutely nobody cares that you lost your child, go to God. He is steadfast. His love is immovable. He is sure. He is always there. Read through the Psalms. Read through the Book of Job. Read about God's love of all mankind. Yes. He loves even you. Especially you.

Friends can help, but they do not always know how. A spouse can help, but is often hurting too badly to offer the kind of strength that you need. But you never need feel total abandonment. Call out to God. He is there. He will help. He will lift you up when you have fallen. And He truly does care. Always. You will never find anyone who cares quite like our God.

Chapter 5

"This Really Did Happen"

> *Has God forgotten to be gracious? Or has He in anger withdrawn His compassion? Then I said, "It is my grief, that the right hand of the Most High has changed"* (Ps. 77: 9-10).

> *You shall know the truth and the truth shall make you free* (John 8:32).

Have you ever had something very painful happen that has taken a while for the pain to register with your brain? Time is actually needed to register the impact of pain that the trauma has caused. A few years ago I walked through our garden one very hot day, and I began to feel little pricks. It took a while for the pain to register, but when it did the pain made me take action quickly. I was receiving multiple bee stings and I didn't even know it while it was happening. The bees had even gone up my pants leg to sting. I cringe yet when I think about that. Bee stings and I do not mix well at all. I ended up in the hospital with a severe reaction. But the amazing thing was that as the bees were stinging I was not fully aware of what was happening. It took a while for the injury, pain, and the result of the injury to all come together.

81

Accident victims will often tell of real horror stories. They may have an arm or leg severed, and after the initial brunt of the pain they feel nothing. They do not even know they are missing a limb until they see the actual disfigurement, or have someone tell them that they are missing a limb. The severe pain releases a numbing effect for a period of time.

Child loss is very similar in nature to these incidents where there is a delay in feeling the complete pain. It takes a while for the mind to grasp hold of child loss, to settle in the mind, and to seem real. Everything seems blurred and there is no real feeling for a brief period of time. You are well aware that something very terrible has happened and when the full impact hits, the pain is severe, The extent of pain from child loss may take several months to actually take its full toll on the heart of a parent. I fully believe this period of numbness is necessary and natural because the pain, if received all at once, would be almost too much to bear. Especially when the child loss comes quickly and quietly, like the unexpected intruder in the night.

I was talking with some teachers at the school where my children attend, and one of them told me of a young mother's recent tragedy. This mother had her little six-month-old daughter safely strapped into her car seat and they were on the way to the baby sitter's house. The baby fell asleep in her car seat. At least that is what this young mother thought. Only, when she went to reach in for the little girl to remove her from her seat, she was totally still. During this brief car ride, this precious little one had died right in the presence of her mother. This happened over five months ago and the full impact of this loss still has not totally hit this young mother and her husband. They are just now beginning to feel the real heartache and pain from this loss. Yes, they know their daughter died. But knowing and being able to say this really did happen are two entirely different things.

In early child loss such as with a miscarriage, stillborn, or even in a Sudden Infant Death Syndrome death, there are many, many phases that parents must go through before finally realizing that their child is forever gone. A mother suffers the physical symptoms of her body changing from a pregnant state back to a non-pregnant state. It is not uncommon for a woman to experience actual kicking sensations of the baby, or for milk production to continue for a period of time. She still may feel extremely tired and experience continued nausea. Her symptoms of pregnancy, even though child loss has occurred, may continue on for some time. Sometimes it takes several months before these physical symptoms stop.

A father who has gone through early child loss may have symptoms of anxiety or depression, total silence, anger, or he may go through a period where he just cannot stay focused on any one thing. Thoughts of this baby that once was the center of attention were taken away so suddenly and it takes a while for the total impact of the loss to really hit.

A mother may still feel the symptoms of pregnancy, but the sad fact remains that she will never feel the baby. Instead, she will be reminded each month of the truth of what happened, when her uterus spills forth its lining, and her body literally weeps. A father may daydream about Little League outings and trips to the park, but these outings are not going to come about. Not with this child that is now gone. I believe that coming to the full realization, the final belief and understanding that child loss has occurred, is probably the most difficult part of all. Until we can actually accept the fact of the child loss, we are at a standstill in time. We may catch an occasional glimpse of the sun, as mentioned in the previous chapter, but until the final acceptance of what is occurs, the sun can never completely break through those clouds. The pain penetrates through to the very soul just thinking about the child loss, blocking the ability to accept what has happened. The "what has happened" in this case is the fact that your child is gone, never coming back.

Early child loss presents a real problem in this area of acceptance. Since a baby was never really held and rocked, you never heard the crying in the night, the diaper changes never took place, there is great difficulty in accepting the finality of early loss. Perhaps this is part of the reason why so many couples try to hurry up and have another child. If another pregnancy occurs soon enough, this period of painful acceptance can be skipped over. I, personally, can attest to this.

When I think back over all of my losses, the losses were never easy. There is intense pain and feelings of emptiness associated with each and every loss. But in all truthfulness, the least painful losses were the ones when I got pregnant within a year after the loss. This final acceptance stage did not have a chance to set in for very long. With a new pregnancy comes new expectations, new hopes, and new joy. A longing again for the future. A break in the clouds. Unfortunately, this does not happen for every couple. For so many, there are not more pregnancies, or the following pregnancy ends in child loss, also. This acceptance that your child has really died is a difficult period of time, to say the least. This actual acceptance can take years to come about. This is why it is so important to have loving friends, family, and health care workers who will allow you to talk through this time of grief. The more often you can verbalize the words, "I lost my child," the sooner the acceptance comes. Hiding behind grief or putting it on the back burner of your mind will eventually take its toll.

Several years ago some close friends of ours wanted desperately to have a baby. They miscarried the first time and it was very disappointing, but several of their friends had miscarried before, and assured them that things would feel better soon, and they would have a little baby in their arms before they knew it. After a few months had passed this couple was expecting another baby. Once again, though, early child loss occurred. Another miscarriage. Another stay in the hospital. Another disappointment. And another trip back home to an empty house. This second miscarriage was more difficult to accept, and they still desperately wanted a baby. After about a year, we got a call from this couple. They were ecstatic. They were expecting a baby, and the first prenatal visit went well. The second prenatal visit also went well. A baby was growing and thriving, and their anticipation of this little one was hard to contain. They had only told their parents so far, besides sharing their good news with us. Now they were to the point of shouting their joy to the world. Then it happened. The hemorrhaging began, and the baby was gone.

My husband went to the hospital immediately when we received the call. I was pregnant at the time, and just felt that it would be too painful for them to see me just yet. I was right. There is a period of time when you just do not want to be reminded that others are having babies when you are experiencing deep pain from your own loss. This couple wept bitter tears. They were at the lowest ebb in their lives. Their dreams and hopes had been shattered once again. They felt as though they had set themselves up for more pain than they could bear. They vowed right there in that hospital room that they would never, ever go through this pain again. And they did not. The reality had set in a bit quicker after each loss.

There was a very simple surgical procedure that could have been performed on my friend to help her carry her next pregnancy to term. She probably would have had to use bed rest, and extra caution, but the doctor felt very sure that they had tracked down the problem, and she could deliver a healthy, beautiful baby. But this couple never did open themselves up to that risk of pain again. The clouds never parted completely, and they got stuck in the dark shadows of grief. They have long since moved away, and we have still remained friends over the years. For them, accepting what was became too much of a burden, and my heart aches every time I think of them.

May I mention that there are help groups available for couples such as this who just never could seem to get life completely back together again. Many cities have groups started by women who have miscarried multiple times. And Compassionate Friends may have served as a great help to a couple like our friends. They felt so alone, so unique in their grief. It would have helped, I am sure, to talk to others who shared the same problems. Instead, this couple withdrew into a shell of silence, and never did fully break the grip of grief.

For parents who have lost an older child, facing the fact that your child is forever gone is such a difficult, burdensome, lonely thing to do. Even after you have grieved and sorrowed for several months, the finality may not yet have hit you totally. This is so sad, because this is the time when most friends and family think it is time to get on in life. They often express to you that it is time to get back to some normal living. They just do not understand how the pain of child loss works. For many parents the fact of child loss is just beginning to seem real. It usually takes several weeks or months to go through all of the different changes we mentioned in Part I of this book. The hurting, the shock, the feeling of being so alone. And that awful feeling that nobody cares. Then, somehow, in some unexpected way, a little flicker of light seeps through the clouds of despair, and you do begin to feel an occasional moment where your whole mind, body, and soul is not preoccupied with thoughts of your child. Right when you think you are finally feeling better, it often hits again like a bombshell. The roof caves in. The cards fall down. You finally realize that the place at the table that is empty is going to stay empty. The bedroom that you left just as it was is not ever going to give peaceful sleep to the child among all of the waiting teddy bears. The toys in the toy box are going to remain quiet. The clothes still hanging in the closet are not going to be worn by your child any more. The visits to the doctor are over. There is no more illness to deal with. But there is no more child to care for either. Facing the finality of loss is so painfully difficult. And child loss is so totally wrong.

This time of coming to a full understanding of child loss is often a time when parents visit the grave site of their child often. Parents may even talk to the child as they visit the cemetery, speaking words that were left unsaid. There is often great healing in this. And while many do not understand, this is not unusual to do at all. It is all a part of coming to full terms with the fact that your child is gone — forever. Reading your child's name on the stone marker helps the loss seem real. This is the beginning of accepting an end.

One mother who lost a 16-year-old son in a car accident said that she tried everything she could think of to help this whole, horrible ordeal seem real. One hour she had an active, healthy son. The next hour she was identifying a still body in the hospital morgue. She cried until there were no more tears. She talked about her son's death to whoever would listen. She packed away his clothes. She attended meetings of Compassionate Friends. But it was not until she visited the cemetery time and time again that it was made solid to her that this loss really did happen. She said that for weeks she made the daily walk to the cemetery, laid a fresh flower on her son's grave, fell to her knees, and cried and cried. When her best friend found out what was going on, she became quite concerned. She really thought this mother was losing her mind. She was not losing her mind at all. She was just beginning to understand that her son was gone. Trying to accept what was. And it was like opening up fresh wounds all over again. To realize that the loss is final is the most difficult of all things to face. There is nothing in the whole world that can change this fact. And it takes a long, long time to come to a full acceptance.

When my teenage sister died, my mother did not handle

any of the grief easily. She was engulfed by dark clouds, and she just could not seem to find her way out. My sister died during the summer. The summer following her death, my mother would load up our lawnmower in the car and go to the cemetery where my sister was buried. She did this several times a week. She would mow the same patch of grass, water the same pansies and petunias, and cry her heart out.

No one understood what she was doing. Neighbors thought that she had gone crazy. My uncle, who lived within eye's view of the cemetery could see my mother from his kitchen window. She would mow that small patch of grass over and over again. He insisted she was having a breakdown. He would often call me and say that someone should come get her and bring her back home. I never did go for her. I always knew that she would be home by dark. In my own way, I think I understood that she needed to be there. She needed to see for herself that this loss was real.

She had not cried all through the funeral, but a year later, when everyone else thought she should be doing fine, the flood-gates opened wide. As time went on, my mother visited the grave site less frequently. She came to a full understanding of the harsh truth. My sister was not coming back. Ever. She was really gone. Coming to the truth about such a loss is not easy. Child loss is a truth that is a lifelong hurt.

What happens when parents lose their older children? My grandmother lost two of her three children when they were in their fifties. She had a terrible time adjusting to this. She seemed to handle the deaths of her three grandchildren much easier. Why was that? Because losing a child is not how life is supposed to go. Her children were supposed to live long, fruitful lives and visit her in her golden years. Instead she buried two of her older children and it was a tragedy that she still is not over.

Most of us would think that losing an older child would be much easier than losing a little toddler. I would never say that child loss of any kind is easy. Or easier. It is always an unnatural order of things for a child to die before the parents. I have several older friends who have lost children in their forties or fifties, and I see just as much sadness, just as much depression and lone-liness, and just as many tears shed over the loss of an older child as I see with the loss of a young child. Sometimes more. As parents and children grow older together, a very special bond of friendship grows along with the natural parental love. The child quite often becomes the parent's best friend. You cook together, you share stories together, you shop together, you take trips together, you work in the garage together. You spend wonderful, happy times together.

A widow lady that I know lost her son when he was 54 years old. He died a very unexpected death, and left behind a wonderful wife and four beautiful children. Just two weeks ago, this mother wept on my shoulder as she told me how much she still misses her son. He used to call her once a day. He took her to all of her doctor's appointments. He helped her with her groceries. But, even more than that, even though he was married, he still kept the mother/son relationship special. My friend adores her son's wife and children. She is especially thankful that they thought it was important for her son to remain a son. What special memories she has of him!

Although she has seen a gradual parting of the clouds in the eight years after her son's death, her words to me recently were, "There are days yet when I still cannot believe that he is gone. It just doesn't seem possible." She knows it is true. The acceptance of his death is what is so hard. It just was not supposed to happen. Not this way. Not now. They had so many wonderful years left to be there for each other.

Another older mother that I knew for many years had a middle-aged daughter that developed a disease known as lupus. As the disease progressed, the daughter's kidney's stopped functioning, and she had to go on daily dialysis. The disease took its toll, and within a year after the dialysis began the daughter died. This daughter's mother suffered tremendously when this death occurred. She wished over and over again that her life had ended, and not her daughter's life. Why? Because children are not supposed to die before their parents. It is just not supposed to happen that way. This elderly mother literally called me every day for consolation. She could not accept the fact that her daughter had died. Yes. She had attended the funeral. Yes. She had been through the crying period. Yes. She began to go on with a bit of normal living. But, no, she could not get through this period of acceptance.

I listened to her day after day as she continuously said, "I just cannot believe that she is gone."

Nothing seemed to help this mother in her deep grief. She had a strong belief in God. She was not angry at God or at anyone. She just missed her daughter. And she could not come to a full acceptance of her daughter's death. My friend died less than two years after her daughter's death. I truly believe her broken heart never healed.

When I talked with several parents who had terminally ill children, I asked them what the most difficult part of the entire loss was. Was it seeing their child suffer before dying? Was it knowing that the child was dying? Was it watching their child suffer and being helpless to do something? Several of the parents expressed to me that there is no one thing that stands out as being the most difficult. The entire process is difficult. Just standing helplessly by as a parent was difficult enough.

One father spoke up and said, "Understanding the reality of death is an excruciating pain. Nothing or no one can change the fact that my little girl is gone. There is a period of time when you feel so completely abandoned. Yes. Even by God." This man's eyes showed the torment that he is feeling from the loss of his daughter. And he is right. No one can really take the pain away.

Coming to an acceptance of what has happened does help, though. I think that acceptance of anything unchangeable is always so difficult. Blindness. Deafness. Paralysis. Divorce. Infertility. These are all terribly difficult things to deal with. And there are more. In fact, we could probably fill pages with such heartache situations.

Child loss seems to fall into a category all its own, though. After the shock. After the loneliness. After the initial hurting. Right about when you get to feeling that maybe, just maybe, life can continue on, comes the part of facing the truth head-on. Really, truly understanding that this is one situation that is irreversible. This loss is a permanent loss comparable to none other.

In the book *The Kennedy Women* Jackie Kennedy seemed to be rushed through the period of grief that she needed to come to a full realization of what had really happened. She needed time; time was not an allotment given to her. The competitiveness of childbearing in the Kennedy family was friendly, but real. I see it in families today all of the time. Brothers and sisters comparing pregnancies, babies, children's intelligence, and such. For such a well-known person as Mrs. Kennedy, there must have been a tremendous pressure put on her to rush through her losses and try to have another baby again. She needed to keep up with the Kennedy tradition of having large families. When she lost her son Patrick, I think it was just too much for her. She finally had to face the fact that she lost several children. Different accounts written about Jackie Kennedy speak of her moods, her depression, her crazy spending sprees, her often whimsical behavior. I wonder if it all had to do with coming to terms with her losses. It was the moment of truth that seemed to be so harsh for her. Her life changed dramatically when she finally came to terms with her losses.

A lot of parents reach this point of acceptance about what really happened and they begin to place blame. This is a common thing that most of us go through. This is especially true if something bad such as child loss happens to what we term "good people." Those people who praise and worship God continuously. Those people who would help anyone. Those people who give so much of themselves to others. Christians. Unfortunately, somehow we have gotten the notion that bad things do not happen to believers. God never, ever promised that. If we read and study the Bible, we see that terrible circumstances often came to those who loved Him the most.

Satan loves to plant these little seeds of doubt and misunderstanding in our minds. And, so often these seeds grow into a full blooming anger at God. When parents finally realize that God is not going to bring this child back, many point an accusing finger at God. This is a dangerous place to be in our belief, because it will hinder us from ever truly accepting what has happened, and finally being able to continue on in this life.

One woman shared her anger at God with me quite openly. She said that she lost three babies in a row to early child loss, then went on and delivered a stillborn son. She was a godly woman, totally devastated by her losses, but totally trusting in God. Until . . . the stillbirth. That, she felt, was a completely cruel act of God. She could find no purpose, no real reason for God putting her through this pain. She said that she felt as though God has made a mockery of her faith. She had trusted Him to do what was best, and He had taken four children from her.

It is now six years since the stillbirth, and I am happy to say that this lady's anger with God is gone. What helped her the most? First and foremost, the constant comfort she received from her husband. She said he hurt. He cried. He went through a period of deep despondency and grief.

But, he never lashed out at God. She said that he constantly reminded her that God did not do this to them. And, as long as she remained angry with God, evil was winning this battle. It took this woman four long, difficult, lonely years to get to the point where she fully understood. She could finally say that this really did happen. And, along with that, she understood that anger at God would not change a thing. No amount of anger would change the fact that she had lost four children. Some people handle this coming to the truth better than others. This lady had a most difficult time. She had some terribly difficult hurts to face. It took her several years to get past this anger, disappointment, and hurt, and to finally accept the finality of it all. Was she a weak person? Was she a person that was ready to go off the deep end? Was she a selfish person, believing that God owed her some special blessings? No. Not at all. She was a beautiful lady longing to have a precious baby with the husband that she so dearly loved. She wanted to complete the family unit by having a baby. Her longings were normal — in fact, God-given. She was not a terrible person. She was simply a lady having many problems coming to a full acceptance of so many losses. One loss is difficult enough to bear. This lady had to come to terms with several losses. She needed lots of love, patience, and time.

In the book *Worry-Free Living* there is an entire section devoted to coming to terms with the truth. Until a parent gets beyond the initial shock and the first stages of grief, and to a full understanding of what has really happened, the healing of the heart cannot begin. Maybe this is why fathers seem to come to terms a little quicker than mothers. And oftentimes, a little more completely. Most men, by nature, are just more able to look at something as defying as death — the loss of a child — and understand that it really happened. Women tend to cling more tightly to what they wish really was, rather than face the painful truth.

I had a friend who actually caught her husband in bed with her best friend, told me about it, and then went on for weeks as though nothing unusual had happened. It was not that she did not understand what had happened. She just did not have the strength in her to face the crushing facts. Not yet. Child loss is very much like this for many women. They may actually talk for months as though the child is just away, about to come home any day. This is just a pretense. A putting off of the truth until a stronger time — a time when both her body and soul can face the blunt, cruel facts of child loss.

For parents of missing children, this is a terrifying process to go through. How does a parent deal with the missing child and the strong possibility of the death of that child? It is wrenching enough to go to bed every night not knowing where your child is, or not knowing what happened to your child. John Walsh could not even begin to face the fact until he had some answers about his son Adam. Yes. He knew his son was missing. Of course he and his wife knew that. But they had a double grief to bear. They also had to deal with "not knowing." The not knowing what happened to their son. Once they learned of Adam's death, they could begin to face the cold, stark fact that this nightmare really did happen. Eventually the Walshes were able to accept the fact that Adam was never coming back. On paper, this sounds like such an easy thing to do. It is by no means easy. It is a grueling thing to have to go through. A horror that cannot even begin to be put down on paper. But the fact remains that until the Walshes came to accept and understand what had happened (not "why"), they could not begin to heal. There could be no real break in the clouds of grief and despair, only momentary flickers of light.

Again, my heart aches deeply for those parents who must live with the ongoing trauma of having a missing child. Fear would overplay grief in this type of child loss, I am sure. The fear of what might be. Where is my child right now? Understanding what really happened — that your child really and truly is missing — can be one of life's greatest torments. There can be no peace, no beginning to go on, until everything is placed into the hands of God. I just do not see how it could be humanly possible to face the fact that your child is missing without the miraculous peace that passes all understanding that only God can give. God promises that He will grant a peace beyond all understanding. Philippians 4:7 says: "And the peace of God, which surpasses all comprehension, shall guard your hearts and your minds in Christ Jesus." This is a time when I am sure that parents must learn to trust that promise of God.

The timing is never right for the death of a child, at least not by our human understanding. There is a fine Christian lady who talks of the death of her son Chris. He was killed by a motorist while he was riding his bicycle, delivering newspapers. He was the kind of teen that every parent dreams about. He was an honor student in school, he was faithful to God, and he worked hard at home. He was respectful, and lots of fun. He just was your model child. Life was wonderful for this family, until that dark day when this mother received the phone call that every parent wishes they would never receive. "There has been an accident, and it doesn't look good. You'd better come to the hospital right away." Chris lived for only two hours. The parents of this young man went through weeks and weeks of the most grievous kind of suffering and disbelief. After a period of about a year, they began to be able to move on in life a bit. They both became very active with their jobs and they both volunteered on numerous committees for the neighborhood. Right when they thought that things were going along much better, it happened. There had to be a reckoning with the truth. In order for them to move on in life, they had to accept the fact that their Chris was never coming back home. Ever.

This family had a real tough time believing that Chris' death was real. Bad things just do not happen to kids like Chris. Their son should have lived. He had so much to give to so many. But he had died, and now they were left to face the harsh reality of it all. Even the words on this paper seem so empty compared to the magnitude of it all. I'm sure they wrestled day and night for months on end with the "why" and "if only" questions. In the final analysis, the fact still remained that their son had died.

It took several years before coming to a full acceptance of Chris's death. These parents faced several bouts of depression while trying to accept what truly was. Once they were able to accept, they were able to go on. Do you see how very important it is to come to terms with the truth? The truth truly is able to set us free. I looked at a picture of Chris the other day. He had a smile that would charm anyone. His eyes seemed to sparkle with life. His very love of life seemed to come through in that picture. I found myself just staring at that young man. I really wish that things like this did not have to happen. It's just not right! But that still doesn't change the fact that every day there are young men and women just as precious as Chris that die. This earthly life can be so very, very painful.

What happens to married couples during this period of acceptance of the truth? What if one parent is able to face the child loss and the other cannot? What if one sinks into a depression and the other seems to be able to go on? What if one can talk about what has happened, and one cannot? What if the timing of acceptance is all off?

Please be reassured that very rarely do a mother and father understand and accept the truth of their child's death at the same time or in the same way. Because of so many variables in the relationship with the child, this may be a totally independent process for each parent to go through. In fact, in my talking with many, many parents who have lost a child, not once did I hear them talk about coming to the full acceptance of their child's death at the same time. It is not something you can put your finger on, or mark on the calendar. It is not something you can say happened overnight. It is a process — a slow, eventual process which takes time, understanding and patience. And tears. This may be a time that seems almost like a setback. Just when you thought you were beginning to see the sunshine on parts of your life, your heart begins to break again. This may be particularly difficult for a married couple in their grief. The ins and outs of grief are not easy to deal with. The mood swings and the battles to be fought are most difficult. It is a strained time for a marriage. It is a time when all of your resources should be focused on staying together throughout this great difficulty. Sorrowfully, many couples give in to anger, resentment, the inability to forgive, and the frustration of the daily battles of grief, and they go their separate ways. It's just plain tough to hang in there during these difficult times!

A husband that I know went through a very tragic loss several years ago. He attended hospice meetings, and a few meetings of Compassionate Friends. He also sought individual counseling. Within less than a year he fully understood the loss he had endured. By that, I mean that he was able to accept what had happened. Cancer had ravaged the body of the one he loved so much, and in a year her life was gone. A child was taken. His wife was always a hopeful optimist which is a wonderful quality to possess. However, unrealistic optimism often inhibits reality at a time when it is most needed. This mother had a real problem with the acceptance of her child's death. Somehow, some way, she evaded the topic. She thought that things would be okay. The frustration in marriage came out in the forms of anger, irrational behavior, disappointment with each other, and a time of direct anger with God. This optimistic mother truly believed, even as death was imminent, that a miracle would take place and her daughter would get out of bed and be well. This did not happen. This child did die. She lived a few months longer than the doctors thought she would.

But, ultimately, finally, she died. Am I saying that the mother had no right to be thinking positively? Absolutely not! Quite the contrary. Her optimism no doubt held her through many difficult days. But, when death was inevitable she simply would not face the truth of what was happening, This ended up causing many rifts in the marriage as a result.

The husband went for individual counseling. He needed to know how to continue on in life, when his wife was stuck in the total disbelief of what had happened. This man spent several years patiently helping his wife to slowly come to terms with the cruel fact of their child's death. He was ready to embrace life and to move on. She was lost in a drowning sea of disbelief. She did not want to be near children; he loved the enthusiasm of young life. She would not mention her child's death; he talked of the death constantly. He smiled often; she cried always. They had some real problems to overcome in this marriage. The timing was all off for them. They were not walking down this path of child loss together. They had hit a time in their lives when they were just worlds apart.

Many husbands would have taken the easy road and walked right out the door. This husband wanted to go on in spite of what had happened. His wife had no world because of what had happened. Many difficult days were in the future. Had this husband left his wife at this crucial time, I do believe that he would have been strong enough to survive. But I do not think this wife could have made it alone. She needed the love and patience of someone close by her side to help her understand what had happened. She had always expected the best; the best did not happen this time. Her child had died. The pain seared her heart. This was one thing that an upbeat attitude could not change. She could not bring her child back All of the optimism in the world could not change that one fact that her child was gone. It took a long time for this mother to come to a full understanding of the truth. And what a blessing her husband proved to be. He helped pull her from the clouds of despair to the reality of life. She finally understood what had happened, and the truth had set her free.

It is so very important for husbands and wives to share their true feelings during this time of coming to know the truth. When one is down, the other can help be a strength. This is how marriage is supposed to be anyway. Wouldn't it be a way of drawing even closer if we shared our deepest feelings with the one we love? I truly believe that some couples have come through child loss much stronger people, much closer in their relationship, because of the intimate bond that they have shared during their time of grief. Why do we seem to want to mask our real feelings so often with our mate? Love bears all things; love will certainly bear grief.

This coming to a full acceptance of the fact that child loss has really occurred is a time for getting very practical in your everyday living. The bottom line we want to know is what really helps? What will finally help us get going in the right direction again? How can I regain some enthusiasm for life when life has been taken away? Couples need to work together in this area of grief. Sometimes just getting out of the house together, taking a walk, may help. I visited a husband not too long ago whose son had been killed in a car accident. He was having a terrible time with his wife. She wouldn't even get up in the morning and get dressed. She finally came to the realization that her son had died, and she wanted to die, too. This man, so gentle in nature, asked me to wait in the other room while he helped his wife dress. He ran a comb through her hair as she softly cried. Then he brought her into the kitchen to talk with me. She just wrung her hands and said she wanted to go back to bed. He simply said, "Now, Mother, we are going on a nice walk to look at all of the pretty flowers. It will do you good to get out of the house." He was right, it would do her good. He was right on track for helping her.

Looking ahead always seems to help. When we lose sight of the future, we lose sight of life. Many times it takes forcing ourselves to look ahead. Maybe we can only look one hour ahead today, but it is a step in the right direction. Eventually, ever so slowly, you will find yourself talking about things in the future. That is certainly a sign that you have come to the full acceptance of what is, and you are now ready to walk a step forward. Counting your many blessings also helps. It sounds like something so simple to do, but it really does work. At one particularly difficult time in my life after a second trimester miscarriage, I just couldn't seem to accept the fact that I lost this baby. Everything had been going along so well one day, and then the next day the baby was gone. My husband, on the other hand, was ready to smile again. One morning I was crying, being completely impossible. I was just picking at him for everything. I was upset with life and I was taking my vengeance out on my husband. I really did not like him right at that moment because he was not sharing in my sorrow. Finally, he slowly stood up and said, "I want you to remember one thing. You are not the only person who has ever lost a baby. Try counting your blessings instead of your losses." Then he kissed me on the cheek, and left for work. To tell you the truth, I am glad he walked out the door for work just then because that is probably the most angry I had been with him in a long, long time, He hit on a raw nerve. He hit on the truth. I literally felt like throwing something at him as he walked out that door. He was so right in his thinking and I knew it. I also knew that I was going to have to change.

All day long I cried. In between crying, I yelled. I don't know who I was yelling to — the cupboards, I suppose. I rearranged furniture. I slammed a few doors. And then I cried out to God. My husband was so very right, and I knew it. In his wisdom, he knew that I needed to gently hear those words. I had withdrawn into a lonely world of my own grief. I could not see beyond the perimeters of the grief. I needed that reminder that I was not alone. Others had suffered such sorrow and survived. I would, too. I had to. I wanted to. I needed to. Those few words spoken by my husband from love at the right moment helped me get back to life. Facing the truth and accepting what had happened was the beginning of my walk away from grief. Thank God for my husband. Thank God for my many blessings. And thank God for the small things that mean so much.

This is also a time for a husband and wife to remain physically close. Grief is often a period when the physical relationship in a marriage suffers. So often there is a strong desire to push your mate away, to shut your mate from your life. Inwardly, you may believe that if you enjoy physical intimacy you will be taking a step away from grieving, and that would somehow be wrong.

Nothing could be further from the truth. Even if you are on different levels of grief, you should remain physically close together in your marriage relationship. This is another way of communicating deep commitment and love. Pull towards one another; never push away. Pushing away from each other physically will only widen the barriers that may already be forming. Hold on to each other. Open your heart to love. Grief tends to close the chambers of the heart in order to protect it from further hurt. It is important for husbands and wives to keep their hearts open and receptive to each other. Keeping the marriage bed alive tends to help one feel loved and to give love once again. Even in child loss. Especially during times of difficulties from child loss.

Looking together at pictures of your child may also help. This is not possible for those who have gone through early child loss. However, talking about future dreams does seem to help. It is always quieting to remember special moments together. Talk about those plans you had made for you and your child. Cry about them. And, then hold onto each other and comfort one another.

Facing the truth together is not nearly as difficult as facing it alone. If you lost an older child, remember special happy times spent together. Do not dwell on the difficult times you may have had. No relationship is 100 percent perfect. Your relationship with your child was not perfect, either. Forget the bad times; remember happily the good times. It helps. Sometimes just knowing that no one can take away your special memories with your child helps. This is something so special that you, and you alone, shared. Find comfort in remembering.

Chances are that looking at pictures, remembering good times, and talking about special moments will incite conversation between you as a husband and wife. And even though the conversation may prompt tears, you will also be forced to accept the truth. Always remind yourself, as hard as it seems, that the truth will eventually free you of your deepest burden of grief.

The truth. It hurts so bad sometimes — most times when it concerns child loss. It just does not seem right. It never feels right. It is not right when children die before their parents. But, the

· ·

truth is that it happens. It happens every day. In some small, remote way just knowing we are not alone offers a bit of comfort.

By now your mind may be wandering, and your heart may still be heavy. You are left with that burning question, "What really helps?" Surely it takes more than a visit to the cemetery or a walk in the park. There has to be more than talking, crying, and looking at pictures. It is fine to visit help groups and talk with others. But at the end of the day when the sky turns dark and your heart feels so heavy, there has to be something there to offer more help.

One evening several years ago, I was having a sleepless night and I went into the living room and closed the door behind me. I didn't want to wake my husband. I felt I needed to be alone in my grief for a while. I needed to cry and not feel guilty for doing so. I needed to think sad, lonely thoughts about the babies I had lost, and not be judged for thinking these thoughts. I needed to come to terms with the fact that I was not pregnant. I had lost another child. A child that I really wanted. A child that I truly loved.

As I pulled out the couch and made it into a bed, my body felt cold and so alone. I wanted to be wrapped in comfort and love. I just wanted to share my deepest feelings with someone and not feel like I was a weak person for not handling child loss any better than this. It was those hours at night when the house was so quiet that my pillow would often become soaked in tears. Why? Because that is when I was alone with my thoughts. I was forced to face the truth when I was all alone.

On this particular night, I could hear my husband's deep, peaceful breathing through the walls. And I openly confess that I resented that. Some of you may judge me for feeling that way. Others will completely understand. I held the pillow up to my face and cried into it to stifle my sobs. The more I cried, the more I heard my husband's peaceful breathing. And it bothered me to think that he could sleep so peacefully while I was hurting so badly.

As I was crying that evening, the hours clicked by and I became anxious and fearful. I was so afraid that I would turn resentful towards life. I was afraid that I would never stop hurting. I was afraid that I would never have a smile on my heart again. I was just afraid.

I got up to get some tissues from the bathroom. It was 3:00 in the morning. I looked in the mirror and I looked a mess. My eyes were red and swollen. My lips were parched and dry. I looked like I needed help. I finally decided to do what I should have done a long, long time ago. I reached for my Bible and I went back to the living room. I began reading from the Psalms of David. I read about his cries to God for help. I continued to read. David's heart had been broken just like mine was broken. On that particular evening I could have penned the words of the Psalmist myself.

I continued to read from the Psalms until daybreak. My head was throbbing. My eyes were swollen almost shut. But my heart had been touched. My burden had been lifted. Someone cared. There was someone listening all along. I never had been alone. "Whom have I in heaven but Thee? And besides Thee, I desire nothing on earth" (Ps. 73:25). My God heard my cries, and he answered me. "I waited patiently for the Lord; and He inclined to me, and heard my cry" (Ps. 40:1). My God truly cared. "But Thou, O Lord, art a shield about me, My glory and the One who lifts my head" (Ps. 3:3). In my anguish, I turned to the only one who could fully understand. "When I remember Thee on my bed, I meditate in the night watches, for Thou has been my help, and in the shadow of Thy wings I sing for joy" (Ps. 63:6). He had been there by my side all the time, He was just waiting for me to call out to Him. "I sought the Lord, and He answered me, and delivered me from all my fears" (Ps. 34:4).

There comes a point in everyone's life when you must face God totally alone in that darkest hour. Just you and God. It is at that point of understanding the truth of who God really is, that your understanding of life and death, good and evil, will occur. Satan had held a grip on me. As long as I did not give my all, including my grief, Satan held a power over me. When, in my pain and hurt, I turned to God, and turned it all over to God, I was able to understand. Death was not the end. It was not the final blow. "O death, where is your victory? O death, where is your sting?" (1 Cor. 15:55). I would one day be reunited with my children. I understood, I finally understood. "Because Thy lovingkindness is better than life, my lips will praise Thee" (Ps. 63:3). Rest, peaceful rest, would come at last.

Chapter 6

People Care; They Just Don't Understand

Because of my wounds, my friends and neighbors avoid me, and my relatives stay far away (Ps. 38:11).

There are so very many tragic circumstances that happen in this life, and many times it seems as though our woes fall on deaf ears. It just seems like people do not even care. They may listen while their minds are drifting off in a hundred other directions, and then just give us a blank stare. The message comes through to us loud and clear. "What exactly was that? I didn't really catch all that you were saying."

We have all experienced this type of thing, probably from childhood on up through our adult years. A small child falls down, gets hurt, and comes screaming for some consolation. If we are in the mood we may stop what we are doing, scoop the child up into our arms, hug and kiss the hurt, get out the bandaids, and stay with the child until the pain stops. On the other hand, if we're in the middle of balancing the checkbook, or in the middle of an important telephone call, we may shoo the child away. "Go wash off your cut, you'll be okay," is about all we can say. We have all had this done to us; we are all probably guilty of doing this to someone at some time in our lives. Maybe that is the way we handle all problems when we have them.

When I was 18 years old and living away at college, I remember having what I thought to be an urgent problem. I really needed to talk to my dad about this. I wanted to go on a trip to Dallas, and I had to have his signed permission by the weekend. I had tried getting his signed permission through the mail. That did not work. No answer. So I drove home to get him to sign the paper. He was so busy with his own work, meeting this person and that person, that I could not stop him long enough to talk. So finally on Saturday, I went into his place of work and made an appointment with the secretary to see my own father. I waited my turn, and he was somewhat furious with me for embarrassing him like that. I did get my permission paper signed, and I was on my way. It was a good learning lesson for me. He did not understand the importance of meeting the deadline of having the paper signed. He did not understand that I wanted to talk with him. And because he did not understand, he acted as though he did not care.

I have watched parents turn their children away time and time again when they have some exciting news to share, or when they have an upset that they really need to talk about. We seem to be especially good at doing this to our children during their young years when they so willingly want to come share everything with us. Far too often we do not share our child's enthusiasm for an accomplishment. Those first hand-drawn pictures or cards that say "I love you." Those first attempts at using scissors and cutting out a picture. We tend to keep looking down as we mumble, "That's nice," while our minds are really on the car repair or the lawn we need to mow. If turned away often enough, children learn not to bother us. They keep their joys and their sorrows to themselves.

The older we get, the wiser we become, especially in the areas of relationships. It is extremely important to be a good listener. Listening, really hearing what is being said, is the beginning to understanding.

Is it any wonder that we have so many silent people? It all begins way back in those early years. Unfortunately, as adults we even do this with our adult friends. We seem to have lost the art of sharing in people's lives — really sharing in their true joys and sorrows. Really caring. One of the most fascinating books I have read on this idea of caring is the book *We Had Everything but Money*. This book was written about the Great Depression days in our country. Reading this book held me spellbound. People really knew how to genuinely care. It was not unusual for people to share their last sack of flour or their last dozen eggs with their neighbors. It was not at all unusual to put up friends or family in your home for an extended period of time. If you were fortunate enough to have a home, you shared what you had.

Some of the most touching stories to me were about those husbands and fathers who would wait in lines every day that were blocks long, just to get a few hours of work. When a neighbor or friend was cut off in line, and got no work for that day, it was not out of the ordinary for the working man to share his wages with the family that was down and out.

Neighbors knew what it was like to be neighborly. They listened; they cared. And, they understood. This thought was carried over when there was a death in the family, also. During those days, many children died of pneumonia, scarlet fever, measles, typhoid, polio, and such. Childhood diseases were devastating. Child loss occurred frequently. People were more aware of the pain of child loss because so many families were affected by such losses. Maybe that's why it was just a bit easier for people — family and friends — to show their love and concern during child loss. They understood what it was all about.

Today, thanks to the wonders of modern medicine, so much child loss has been eliminated. We discussed this briefly in Part I of this book. We have vaccines for diseases that used to carry a death threat. We have surgeries that can now be performed on babies while still in the uterus. These techniques are being updated every day. We have trauma units, respirators, transplants, and chemotherapy. This is just to name a few of the things that have transpired in a very short period of time. All of this has greatly affected the number of children that die in this country each year. But . . . we still do have incurable diseases. We still have accidents that result in death. We still have Sudden Infant Death Syndrome. We still have miscarriages and stillborn babies. We still have babies born with terrible birth defects that result in death. In other words, we have not eliminated child loss. Not at all.

While child loss may not be quite as common as it was 50

years ago, the pain that is associated with child loss is still filled with as much anguish. In some ways, maybe the pain is worse for us today. We expect so much more of doctors and medicine. Somehow, we have the mistaken notion that doctors stand in line next to God. They can cure it all. What a terrible burden to place on our physicians! And, somehow, we think if we just take a pill, it will get all better. That's where this caring and misunderstanding come into full view.

Randy Becton, in his book *Does God Care When We Suffer?* talks about being a healthy young husband and father, not really aware of the pain and suffering that goes on all around us every day of our lives. He tells the story of his personal journey of suffering when diagnosed with incurable cancer, and ultimately how his relationships with everyone, including God, changed dramatically. Randy now cares because he now understands. He knows first hand what chemotherapy is all about. He now knows what huge medical bills mean. He understands what a drain constant visits to doctors and hospitals are all about. He understands exactly what it means to question God. He understands because he has now joined the ranks of the sufferers.

There is absolutely nothing that jolts us into the reality of pain — really understanding that true pain exists — like feeling deep personal pain. You can talk all about it. You can philosophize about it. You can give every explanation possible as to what your personal thoughts on pain are, but until you actually feel some of the fire, things will not completely register. This is similar to telling a young child not to play with fire. We can explain all we want what "hot" means, but until the skin of that child is actually seared, that child will not totally understand the intensity, the depth, the actual pain of the heat.

Trying to get people to understand the intensity of pain that results from child loss is similar to teaching a child that the heat from fire burns. Many people go through life totally clueless for a long period of time about child loss. In fact, child loss will not affect every parent. Not every parent will lose a child. Many, many parents will never know the absolute and unique pain that comes from losing a child, And, it is very difficult to get people on an involved level of caring if they do not understand at all what we are going through.

To truly care, we must at least try to understand. This point comes across so vividly in the area of child loss. While sitting in the intensive care unit of a large hospital with a mother whose daughter was dying, this mother shared some real insights with me. She said, "For the longest while life has been just absolutely wonderful for me. Shopping in quaint antique shops with my daughter. Traveling the world over. Owning a beach-front home. I had it all, and I was so insensitive to the real needs of others."

As this mother's daughter was struggling for life, this lady recalled an event that happened to her on a cruise. The cruise ship stopped on an island noted for its exquisite food and marvelous shopping. However, on that island there were beggars. Lots of them. She remembered a particular sight of a starving mother trying to nurse her starving baby. The islander's hollowed eyes spoke of death. The baby's bloated belly painted a picture that death was near. But this lady speaking to me said that she, along with hundreds of other tourists, turned their heads and their hearts to the beggars and went about their shopping and fine eating.

Now, in her own pain of knowing what it felt like to have a dying child, she was haunted by that island scene. It is so easy to turn our heads when we do not understand. Especially when it comes to something as painful as child loss. We would rather turn our heads away than to be made to feel uncomfortable and have to stare at pain head-on. We would rather not even be reminded that child loss occurs. Child loss is painful just to think about casually, let alone trying to understand what a grieving parent is going through.

You may be wondering at this point why in the world I have gone through such a lengthy explanation of pain, suffering, and understanding. Really, it is quite simple, Most parents who go through child loss do not feel that they have received the help and support over the long haul that they should have received. This is especially true after the first year following the death of a child. Many people act as though they do not even remember your child existed, much less help tend to your hurting soul. This one thing — lack of caring — is probably the single greatest reason why parents who have lost a child grieve so silently. Who is there to listen? Who is there that really understands?

In the beginning of this book, we talked at length about people helping for a brief period of time after child loss and then tending to forget about the pain that is still buried deep within the heart of a parent. For many parents, the end of the first year marks the beginning of the real deep pain of child loss. There has usually been a reckoning with the truth by now. A parent fully understands that the child is not coming back. Ever. That alone is such a painful, terrifying truth to accept.

All around us we look at people laughing, working, tending to the mundane things in life. And sometimes we want to scream so loudly, "I lost my child. Don't you even care?" I really think that people care; they just do not begin to understand. It is s never-ending circle. If people do not understand, how can they possibly care? And, quite often, even when they do care and they do understand, fear keeps them from acting on their compassion. Let me explain this briefly.

When I delivered our stillborn son, it was a totally awkward, uncomfortable thing. It was right after Mother's Day, I knew the baby had already died over two weeks before, and I was waiting for spontaneous labor to occur. All during that time, there was silence from my friends. I do not think that they did not care, although at the time that is how it felt. That is how it seemed. The truth is, no one understood. No one had gone through this same experience. No one had ever come close to going through that same type of child loss Then, when I did deliver the baby, no one knew what to do. We received only four cards. Do you send a sympathy card? Or do you send a card that says, "I hope you are feeling better soon"? Do you send a card of general encouragement? Most people just sent nothing. Did my friends care? Yes. I now believe they did, although at the time I felt like no one really cared. Fear and misunderstanding kept them from doing anything.

What about flowers? There were none. One kind man sent a fruit basket. I will never forget his expression of love. Did people care? I am sure that they did in a general way. But, not deeply. No one had gone through that particular type of child loss. There was no "book of proper etiquette for intra-uterine stillborn deaths" to refer to. My stillborn delivery was a bit different because I actually carried the lifeless baby for so long. I knew well before the delivery that my baby had died.

What do you say? Well, you can probably imagine the awkwardness of seeing a woman with a well-rounded middle, but knowing the baby she is carrying has died. Do you ask, "How do you feel today?" Or, "How did your week go?" Or, "Did you have a great Mother's Day?" The entire situation was a disaster for everyone. No one understood. But I do believe they cared. I can say that only now, after several years, because time has allowed me the benefit of seeing through eyes that are less grieving. Friends cared; they just did not understand. There is no greater teacher than personal pain. That is usually when we begin to see things in an entirely different light.

When an older child dies, the same lack of understanding so often occurs. We seem to get through the bad days somehow, some way, when our child dies. So often, we struggle through those days without much support. But, a year or so later, when our heart is still broken, others really and truly do not understand. Life has moved on for everyone except us it seems. Our friends are back into their routines of everyday living. Jobs, leisure activities, little daily disturbances. Complaining about the usual things such as high taxes, the unbalanced budget, the weather, and such. For the parent who has lost a child, somehow these things are usually not a top-of-the-line priority. We know that these problems are not infinite. They are temporary problems. Taxes will change just like the ebb and tide of the seas. Our appliances will break down, and then get replaced or repaired. Bills will eventually get paid. But child loss. That is totally different. That is a loss that will remain in the heart of a parent forever. Nothing will ever change the fact, Nothing will ever totally heal the damage that was done to the heart. Nothing. Nothing. Nothing. Friends who have not gone through this intimate walk with death will not fully understand. Because they do not fully understand, they cannot deeply care. That is another fact that parents who have gone through child loss must eventually come to terms with. And, during such a fragile time of life, when you really need an understanding heart and listening ears, it is often a small consolation to remind yourself that people just do not understand.

I received a very tender letter recently from an older lady who told me a touching story of child loss. She said that her mother died a few years ago, and right before her mother's death she told her of having a ten-month-old baby sister that died. She was too young to ever remember having a baby sister, and her mother and father had kept this painful event from her for almost

60 years. Why? I am sure the parents were silent because they felt their own children just would not understand, much less truly care. This lady said, "All my mother could do was cry as she told me about my baby sister. She was old in years and dying, and had never really gotten rid of the pain."

Then, she continued on and said, "I've been through a lot of terrible things in life, but I just do not think I could withstand child loss." It was not until this woman had grown children of her own that her mother disclosed the pain of child loss that gnawed at her heart all of those years. I wonder if friends helped her. I have a feeling that most of them had long forgotten the loss of that little ten month old. This mother was still grieving and hurting right up until the very day that she died.

Several years ago I was given a most unusual baby gift. An elderly lady gave me a scratchy, plain, woolen blanket that had been kept in a chest in her attic for well over 30 years. I was a bit taken aback until I heard the story that went along with the blanket. This lady was unable to bear children. Her husband, who had been previously married and widowed, had one child. This only child died of a childhood disease before the age of one. All of those many years, they had hung onto that baby blanket as a final reminder of that precious child. Giving me that blanket was a closing of a chapter for them, a true coming to terms of the truth. I find myself crying as I write about this because I was so uncaring to this couple. I did not understand the magnitude of the gift or that little woolen baby blanket. It represented all of their joy and all of their pain. They wanted me to understand. I did not. Not at all. Not until I lost children of my own. And even then, I could not fully comprehend, because I had the blessing and privilege of having children. This woman was barren; her husband lost his one and only child. I didn't care enough because I just did not understand. I did have the sense to carefully wrap that blanket in tissue paper and place it in my attic.

This couple died before I ever began to realize the depth of their pain. I feel so awful about that. I cared, but not like I should have. How could I? I just did not begin to understand their deep, anguished pain. I will never part with that baby blanket; it serves as a reminder of how truly deep the pain of child loss is. This couple needed friends, caring friends. Instead, no one really understood. Not enough to deeply care. That is part of the pain parents of child loss must also bear. Understanding that people cannot sensitively care until they understand your loss. Unfortunately, a loss that is so deep, so damaging to the heart, so personal, is not ever fully understood by others.

People, our friends, will often say really strange things to parents who have lost a child. They often choose the most inopportune time to say these things, too. Right when we start feeling just a bit better, when we are handling the pain just to the point where we can function a little more normally, someone may say something that really pricks our heart. It is during these times of hurt that we must constantly remember that people say things that are often not the things that we need to hear. They are often things that make the hurt worse rather than help. They are things that never should have been said. These things come from the mouths of those who mean well, but just do not, cannot, fully understand.

Probably the most-used phrase we hear is, "It was God's will that your child died." I am not so sure that parents who have longed for a child, prayed for a child, and then have the child die, are comforted by hearing those words. I am not so sure that they have experienced God's will. Nor am I convinced that parents who have lost a child to a painful terminal illness have been blessed with God's will. I am certainly not convinced that parents of missing children, who agonize every day over the welfare and whereabouts of their child, are consoled by hearing the words, "It is God's will."

I am sure that most of you get the idea of just what I am talking about here. It is not God's will for babies to die. It is not God's will for precious children to be violently taken from their parents. But if we can be convinced that God does such things to us, maybe we can be torn away from the love of God, too. Evil has such a way of deceiving us!

Also, the classic line, "I know just how you feel," is not really appreciated or helpful if the words come from the lips of a parent who has enjoyed healthy pregnancies and no child loss in their own life. How can that person say, "I know how you feel"? One father I know literally comes unglued every time some well-meaning person says this to him about the loss of his daughter. He just does not want to hear those hollow words. People who have healthy, active children running around their homes every day do not know how it feels to have life so harshly snatched away. They do not understand at all the loneliness that now fills the home. They do not understand at all what it feels like to live with a broken heart that will not ever totally be whole again. Those words, "I know how you feel," are best left unsaid if they are coming from the mouth of someone who has never felt their particular pain. Those words offer no real comfort.

Another thing that is often said by people who do not understand child loss is, "Who knows what kind of problems your child would have had? At least now you know your child is in heaven." While these words are true, they certainly are of no consolation for a parent whose child has died. Parents would much rather have a child, problems and all, than no child. That statement makes me hurt from the inside out every time I hear it. It is a statement that is said to mean well, but there has not been much thought put into it, Every grieving parent wants their child alive; there is no comfort found in the death of a child. No one knows what the future holds for their child. But, without the child, there often seems to be no future.

One mother who lost her 50-year-old son was told over and over again that she should be glad that her Jon did not linger on and on with a painful illness before be died. When this older child died, many such comments were made to his wife, his children, and to his mother. The most common response to this young man's death was, "You should count this as such a blessing. He's much better off now." This poor mother became both distraught and irate. She did not feel that her son's death was a blessing. Not at all. She did not feel relieved over his death. What she did feel was sorrow. Deep, deep sorrow over this loss. She felt lonely. She would never see her son again in this life, And she felt that life had gotten all mixed up. She was supposed to die before her son. She was not comforted by the words of those who did not understand. Keep in mind that people mean well, but so many times careless words can do more harm than good.

To those who have suffered child loss by miscarriage or stillbirth, all kinds of comments will be made in an attempt to comfort. Most often are the words "You can always try again." Second to this is "The baby was probably deformed. You wouldn't want to deal with that." And, the always-stated, "Now God has one more angel with him in heaven."

Unfortunately, none of these words even begins to come close to comforting the parents who have longed for a baby. Not everyone can try again to have a child. Many, many times health problems are responsible for the loss. Irreversibly damaged fallopian tubes. Perhaps a uterus has had to be removed. Maybe secondary infertility has set in. Any number of problems may arise.

The real issue is that a baby has died. The parents wanted this baby. Hearing about "trying again" does not offer much help. Not when your heart is breaking. Hearing that the baby may have been deformed is just another way of saying you should be glad that the baby died. You could have had an imperfect child. In rare instances, a parent finds this statement of some comfort, but most often a parent still longs for the child, imperfections and all. In fact, many thousands of children are born with all kinds of deformities each year. And they are dearly loved and cared for. Most parents have an extraordinary ability to love what we would call a "less than perfect" child. I know several parents who have handicapped children, and these children are loved and adored. There is such a lack of understanding in this area of child loss.

Finally, the idea that "God needed one more little angel," so he took your child. I do not read anywhere in my Bible that God hand-picks babies, and kills them, then takes them to heaven because he "needed one more little angel." It is an absolutely beautiful thought to know that our little children have gone on to heaven. And, that, the Bible does tell us. It is a wonderful thought to know that our children will be waiting for us to be reunited once again. But, it is a mistaken notion that God takes our children from us by killing them to be with him. He just does not do that. Death came about because of sin way back in the beginning of time. The death of children is not a way of filling heaven with little angels. Truly, I long for the day when I can see my children in heaven. But, it is not comforting to think that God ended my child's life to take with him. These are all words spoken from well-meaning people, but they are not words spoken from people that understand.

Do you see how difficult this entire dilemma of child loss is? It is so very difficult for everyone. Parents want to talk. Parents need to talk. People so often do not want to listen. When friends do try to talk, they frequently say the wrong things. Then, they intensify the hurt even more. If friends do not talk about the loss of your child, it seems like they do not care. When friends try to care, they often do not understand. How do we get help? Real help. How do we get beyond this circle of grief, silence, hurt, and fear?

I have found that if you do not know what to say, it is probably best not to say anything. A hug. A smile, A warm handshake. A shared tear. A prayer. Those things all help, and they also express what you often cannot say. Probably the all-time worst thing said to me was two days after my stillborn. One of my best friends saw me and said, "It is so great to see how you got your figure back all in one day!". She was nervous. It was a terribly awkward situation. And she just blurted out the first thing that came to her mind. Just a hug would have been sufficient. In fact, a hug from a friend at that moment would have been just wonderful. The words were meant to comfort, but they only added pain. I did not want to look great, I wanted to look fat and pregnant. I wanted my baby.

So, what is a friend supposed to do? What is a friend supposed to say? What is a parent to do? What is a parent to say during this most misunderstood time of child loss? It helps so much for everyone to remember.

In a book I was reading, *The Bereaved Parent*, a statement stood out just as though it was written in bold letters. It said that there is only one thing worse than speaking ill of the dead child and that is not speaking of the child at all. It helps a parent so much to be allowed to talk comfortably around others of their child. Or, in the case of early child loss, the parents should be able to talk of the hopes and dreams that they had for the child. This life, this child, was real. To be forgotten is almost a blasphemy of life itself.

One of my friends related a story to me about two years ago about her mother. She said that on Memorial Day her family always places flowers on the graves of family members who have died. Each year a different family member is in charge of ordering flowers for this occasion. This particular year it was my friend's turn to order the flowers. She ordered flowers for everyone, except for her brother who had only lived a day after birth. He was the first of four children, so she never knew her brother. She never saw him. She even temporarily forgot his name. She could not believe that her mother, now well into her seventies, got so upset over these forgotten flowers.

I tried to explain that this baby was special to her mom and dad. He was their child, their first-born. He was real, and he had died. He had a right to be remembered. My friend just stared blankly at me. She just did not understand. She has healthy children of her own. She never had even a hint of a problem in her pregnancies. She did not begin to think about her mother's pain. How could she? She just did not understand. To her, it seemed almost foolhardy of her mom to place a flower on this child's grave. After all, he only lived one day. She could not even begin to imagine the importance, the significance, the pain, that was held in that one day. My friend's mother wanted to talk, but her words just did not penetrate to the heart of this daughter. So many just do not understand.

Our close friend Doug Lawyer recently visited with three of my children who are living away at college. Doug, my kids, and their friends went out to eat and enjoyed a great evening together. It has been several years since Doug has seen some of my boys, so it was quite a joyous reunion.

All of the kids called home after their time with Doug, and it was interesting to me that they all knew about the death of Doug's young son Dougie. Yes. This happened many years ago — over 40 years now since this little one died. I am sure that Doug knew that my boys could not begin to understand what he had gone through. They could not possibly care deeply enough to minister to Doug. But Doug talked anyway. He needed ears to listen. He needed to remember. He wanted my boys to remember that he had a son. Seeing those young men, my sons, stirred within Doug moments of past anticipation, past hopes, and past dreams for the time when his son would have gone on to college, Doug loves people with a passion. He loves God with his entire being. He is wise enough to understand that people care, even young people. They just do not always understand completely. How can they? Doug has not allowed his heart to become bitter by people's lack of understanding. He has kept his son's memory alive, and will do so until the day they are reunited in heaven.

How can a husband and wife deal with this lack of understanding from friends and family? A husband and wife have so many hills to climb, trails to blaze, and hurdles to jump just when they say the words "I do." Once a child enters their lives, things get even more complicated. Nothing is ever the same anymore. This is another one of those ponderables, unable to be fully understood until you actually have a child of your own.

I absolutely love the humor found in the writings of Erma Bombeck. She has a tremendous talent for saying things that touch the heart and get the point across. And, she does it with humor. In her book *A Marriage Made in Heaven or Too Tired for an Affair* she has several sections written on her parenting days. In the beginning of her marriage, friends all around her were getting pregnant, while nothing happened to her. No pregnancy. No morning sickness. No baby. Finally, a decision was made to adopt a child. Erma and her husband really wanted to become parents. However, they decided not to go crazy decorating a nursery, buying tons of baby accessories, snapping thousands of pictures. They were going to remain sane, and not allow this little one to change their lifestyle. Right? Wrong! They went completely, wildly, madly in love with this precious bundle, their baby. No one could explain it to them. They never completely understood what happened to new parents until they became new parents themselves. It was only then that the lights came on and they finally understood parenthood.

In the last part of Erma's book, she talks about when she became pregnant at the outlandish age of 40. She lists all of the reasons why she really did not want this baby. The timing was just all off. But, the inevitable happened. She fell in love with this child. They were one, as only a mother can fully understand. She tells a bittersweet story of the loss of this child. The doctor discovered that there were no signs of the baby's growth in the fourth month. Erma begged the doctor to just give her a few more weeks with this child. She was one with this baby. How could she now let this part of her go? Sadly, the baby had died, and Erma delivered a dead baby in her sixth month. She no longer used humor in her writing. and her tone was serene, sincere, and touches every human heart.

She loved this baby. Her life was forever changed by this baby. Did everyone understand? Not at all. Her career was just beginning to blossom and grow. Her heart, her very soul, longed for her baby to blossom and grow. Only she and her husband completely understood what she meant when she said there will always be a longing for this child. Had I not experienced child loss myself, that section of her book would have probably seemed pointless to me, The humor was gone. It did not fit in. In reality, though, it not only fit in, but helped explain who Erma is. She is a woman who joined the rank of silent suffering. She is a parent who suffers from child loss. She is a wise, witty woman who had joined hands and hearts with fellow sufferers. She had a heart forever etched in pain. She and her husband now faced new and unique hurdles to climb. And, for the most part, they would do it alone. Friends cared; they just did not even begin to understand.

Since couples have this unique pain, this unique loneliness, this unique hurt that very few people understand, how do they cope? Child loss, like it or not, sets you apart from others. While other couples are concerned with new nursery furniture, weekly soccer games, ballet classes, drama club rehearsals, driver's licenses, and such, your life may be focused on just surviving the hour of the day. Just making it through one day without crying, without hurting. You lost your child. Your world seems all wrong. And nobody seems to understand, much less care. While your friends are fussing over what particular brand of clothing to buy, which theater passes to get, or what place has the best Friday evening buffet to eat, you may be just concerned with making it through the week to Friday evening.

Even though it has been a year or more since the loss of your child, the music still seems off key, the evenings seem far too long, and the food just does not taste like it should. And your friends do not seem to care. They seem to have somehow forgotten you. You are convinced they have forgotten your child. Your child's name no longer comes up in conversation. It is as though your child never even existed. That type of silence hurts so much!

One wife shared with me how her husband was not much of a talker, but he would quietly reach for her hand and simply hold her in the long, dark hours of the night. No words had to be spoken. They just understood. They comforted one another Simply by each other's presence. They would dry each other's tears and never speak a word. A deep love is like that; words are not always necessary. A love that has been pained by child loss understands.

Some of you may be saying that this is all great for the couples that have remained together throughout this long lonely, heartbreaking ordeal. What about the ones who have felt abandoned by friends, and who have actually been abandoned by their mate? Where is the help for them? They have no one to hold them close in the still of the night. There is no one to share an intimate moment with them. There is no one to reach across the room to grasp hold of a hand. There is no one to talk to. There just seems to be no one. And it feels so terrible alone.

My heart truly aches as I think of this type of pain. It is somewhat bearable to think that friends do not care because they do not understand. But, when a mate is no longer there to share the loss of that child, your child, black takes on a whole new meaning. Alone. Alone in grief. Alone in child loss. Alone. There is no pain like that of being alone.

I am remembering back several years ago to the day when my father walked out the door of our home, never to return. My sister had died. That was a loss that would forever touch the very heart of my family. And when my father left our home, it was similar to going through another death. Alone. He would not be there to comfort. He would not be there to talk. He would not be there to give emotional support. He would just not be there. My mother went downhill real fast after he left. She seemed to stop caring. I imagine that is exactly what happened. She had friends, but they did not understand. "Be strong," they said. "Be tough." She was not strong. She was not tough. She lost a daughter and a husband. The two most unique, most intimate types of love to lose. With each loss, she lost part of herself. She just never pulled out of her grief. She became silent after a while. She depended on alcohol to numb the pain, and her eyes grew dim. Grief closed the window of her heart. She pulled into a shell of grief and sorrow, and never did come out. It seemed like no one really cared. I do not think a soul that knew her really understood. It is just now that I am beginning to understand. I just wish I had understood sooner.

What does help a parent who is so alone in grief? Others cannot help if they do not understand. Words are often meaningless. When your mate is gone you have lost your best friend. What a feeling to have lost all feeling. Life just seems so very alone.

This past Christmas my younger sister and I were talking about getting together on Christmas Eve. She somehow got on the subject of our sister that had died. "That must have been awful for you," she said. "I don't remember much at all, but it must have really been hard to go through."

I found myself totally unable to talk. It was not something that was just awful. It was not just something that happened in the past and is now over. It is still just awful. I find myself crying, missing my sister more now than I did years ago. It is awful. It will always be awful. But even worse is the fact that so few understand. My husband and children never knew my sister. So they cannot help. My mother has died. She cannot help. My father is gone. No one can remember my sister with me. It is such an alone feeling. I remember so much about her, but no one else does. She is not real to anyone but me. I am her sister. She was real and no one even remembers.

I am sure that this type of alone grief is intensified a hundred times over for a parent. What really helps? For me, just remembering. Remembering the times I had with my sister. And thinking of seeing her again some day. Sometimes just watching others her age helps. I now have a daughter who is the age my sister was when she died — 13. I see new life all around me, and that helps. It helps to understand that this life is only temporary. Evil will not be forever. These things all help during those terribly lonely hours. But, I know, too, that the pain will never completely go away. Love binds hearts together forever. Even death cannot break the bond of love. God designed love to be that strong. Even if hundreds of people remembered and cared. Even if I could talk of my sister and remember old times. Even if people totally understood. There would still be an empty spot, an ache in the heart that will not go away. Child loss is like that. That is all part of the uniqueness of this type of loss.

Maybe God designed a parent's love for a child to be that way. Maybe. Just maybe we are always supposed to have a small ache that reminds us to long for the future, Maybe that is just how it is supposed to be.

Every person who has gone through child loss experiences deep personal pain. For some, the pain is relentless, such as the continuous pain associated with a missing child. For some there is an anger that begins building because, as we face the truth, we know that child loss is not something that will go away in the morning. Pain. Anger. Solitude. Abandonment. Loss. All familiar words to the one who has lost a child. In the end, we are left asking the question as the psalmist David did, "Who really cares?"

It is at this point of feeling so alone, so abandoned, so misunderstood, so uncared for, that we need to remind ourselves that someone does care. It takes a tremendous amount of faith, sometimes an actual forcing, to say that God cares. Whether we have friends or not, whether we have a mate or not, sooner or later aloneness will set in. And that is when we need the loving help of God more than ever before. When we are shattered by child loss, when we are feeling so alone, when we feel deserted by everyone on earth, we need to turn our thoughts towards God. Why? Because if we do not turn towards God, eventually we will turn away from Him. When we turn away from God, we have not allowed God to be God. Think about all of His promises. They are everlasting and sure. There is help and comfort. We may not have a person to sit by our side in our alone times and deepest grief, but we always have God. What an awesome thought! God is always near.

Psalm 34:18 says: "The Lord is near to the brokenhearted, and saves those who are crushed in spirit." God will show his compassion on us in our loneliness and distress. "Thou, O Lord, will not withhold Thy compassion from me; Thy lovingkindness and Thy truth will continually preserve me" (Ps. 40:11). God always cares and he will always stay near to help. "Cast your burden upon the Lord, and He will sustain you; He will never allow the righteous to be shaken" (Ps. 56:22).

Sometimes we just feel we can no longer go on in this life without our child. The pain is just too great. God speaks to us again. God says he will carry our burden. "Blessed be the Lord, who daily bears our burden" (Ps. 68:19). God is the only one who can truly, completely understand each of us and deeply care. People will inevitably fail us simply because of being human in nature. God's love will never fail. He will never leave or forsake us. Psalms 25:1 says: "To Thee, O Lord, I lift up my soul. O my God, in Thee I trust." Are we weak when we cry out to God and question? Maybe. Does God understand? Always. Read the cries of David in the depths of his aloneness and despair. He often wondered where God was. In his wondering he found solace and comfort. And you will, too.

When we feel so alone in our grief, when we need a listening ear, when we want to talk — we need to turn to God. May we truly remember that God is in control. Yes. Even in a situation as lonely, as sad, as devastating as the loss of our child. He will never, ever leave us alone in our grief. God's love is everlasting and sure.

May we not stop loving others; rather, may we, in our own deep grief, love even more. May we grow stronger as we lean on the strength found only in God. "In God I have put my trust, I shall not be afraid. What can man do to me?" (Ps. 56:11). May we always remember that God sorrows with us. We are not alone in our grief. Ever. Psalm 61:4 "Let me dwell in Thy tent forever; Let me take refuge in the shelter of Thy wings" (Ps. 61:4). We have a friend and companion who truly cares. May we feel the arms of God wrap around us and bathe us in His love. It is time. Finally. It is time to share our grief. Our grief is just too heavy a burden to carry all alone.

Be gracious to me, O Lord, for I am in distress; My eye is wasted away from my soul and my body also (Ps. 31:9).

Chapter 7

"I Still Wish I Had My Child"

Have you ever had something bad happen, and you finally accept things as they are, only to drop back into your feelings of wishing that things were different? If we are honest, we have all probably gone through numerous experiences such as this. Maybe we have been invaded by cancer, a leg is removed, and the cancer is declared not just in remission, but cured. We have gone on in life, happy to be just alive. We tell others of all that we have learned from this life-changing experience. We talk of how much we have grown. Our perspective on life has changed. Our priorities are different now. Then one day, sitting on the edge of the bed, attaching the fake leg, it hits us. And it hits hard. And we cry out loudly that we wish it had never happened. We did not need to grow. Not this way. We still wish we had never known cancer. We wish we still had our leg. Lingering in the shadows of the heart are the feelings of pain, and we long for how life used to be.

This often happens in the area of finances, too. I read about it all of the time. People finally make it big. They invest money. They make some smart moves. Buy some investment properties. They make more money. Lots of it. They feel secure. All of life seems great.

Then it happens. Wiped out. Finances are gone. Broke.

Homeless. Time to begin over. A success story gone sour. Now it's time for the burdensome climb from the pit back to the top.

I just recently read such a story in *Guideposts* magazine. This particular man finally made it out of homelessness, got a great job, and has devoted his life to helping others. He learned some real painful life lessons along the way. I wonder if he ever wishes that he could have escaped the pain part, and just kept on making money and helping people. He was always a kind man, long before he became homeless. Why did he have to go through all of that pain? I am sure that he has asked God that question many times over. I am sure that he has occasionally looked back and wished that things could have been different. I am sure that he wishes that parts of his life could have been left alone. Many, many of you who have endured severe hardships, crushing blows to the spirit, know exactly what I am talking about.

Parents go through so many ups and downs when they lose a child that often they cannot keep up with the grief. One day without tears, two days of sobbing. One week of normal living, then a day of anger and bitter tears. One moment of feeling loved followed by several days of feeling so alone. After about a year the grief seems to calm down a bit. You have come to understand your loss — not particularly "why" you had to go through such loss — but you begin to slowly cope. That glimpse of the sun that we talked about previously seems to appear more and more frequently.

Sometimes you find yourself smiling for no apparent reason, and it feels so, so good. The heavy weight of grief upon your heart has been lifting, ever so slowly. You can now go to work, and your mind may get through most of the day without thinking of your child. You may take a walk in the park, see children playing, and not burst into tears. Maybe you can now go out to dinner and have a good time. Yes! The sun is beginning to shine.

And the warmth of the sun on your heart feels so very good.

Then, out of the clear blue, it happens. Grief hits again. And you are knocked flat on your face in anguish. It finally registers again that your child is gone — really gone. It is like a neon sign that flashes in a bright glow: "Your child is gone!" Oh, the pain is crushing. It hits so hard that it takes your breath away. You are left wishing, longing, hoping, for the things that were.

Wanting things to be like they used to be. And yet despair is added to grief. Instead of comfort, there is unrest. Instead of a smile, only tears will fall. Instead of a mended heart, a heart that is torn in two. Again. It is happening all over again.

You probably wonder if this step backwards in grief is normal, or is it just you not being able to handle this loss. Rest assured, you are quite normal. These are feelings that most everyone goes through. Many times we put on a masked front and try to convince everyone that we are okay. I do not really understand why we are so afraid to say that we are hurting. I guess it is just better to look like a conqueror, rather than one who feels conquered.

Grief is such an up and down thing that it is really important to understand the devastation that it can play on your heart. I talked with a young mother who lost a twin. She delivered a set of twin girls prematurely 11 years ago. One little girl lived; the other did not live. This mother is still struggling with this up and down backward longing for her little girl. She seemed to crumble when she told me about the little twin that died. She said that even after so many years she often wishes it never had happened. Did she face the truth of her daughter's death? Yes. Does she have happy days? Yes. She is not totally buried under the heavy clouds of grief anymore. Does she understand that she is not alone in her grief? Yes. She has friends and family that care.

Does she appreciate the blessing of the little girl that lived? Definitely yes. She loves her with all of her heart. Does she still go through times when she wishes that she was pregnant again, and the twins both lived? Yes. Yes. Yes. She wishes her little girl had never died. Will this part of her grief ever end? Maybe. Maybe not. I do not know. That is just how grief is. That is especially how the pain of child loss is.

When my sister died, there was a period of calm about a year and a half after her death. Everything resurfaced though when I reached age 18 and was ready to leave home for college. Grief had hit my mother worse at that time than at any time before. She really longed for my sister. She would have been 16 years old then. Old enough to drive. Old enough to date.

Old enough to have a part-time job. Old enough to . . . just old enough to be. I was leaving for school. I never understood my mother's reaction to my leaving. She would have nothing to do with me. She never said goodbye. She never helped me get ready for school. She never wished me well. She never wanted me to leave. Why? Grief had come back full force again. Just when she thought she was doing better, everything got terribly worse.

Months later, during one of our rare moments of talking, my mother said that she was so afraid of losing another child. She missed my sister so! She just wished that things could have turned out so differently. She wished that she never had to see her child die. My sister had been so sick, but my mother would have given anything to have her back. She knew it could never be the same again. But, oh how grief makes you wish that your child was never taken away. Life could have, life should have, been so very, very different. Children are just not supposed to die before their parents. They are just not supposed to go away and never return.

I worked with a lady that went through several miscarriages in a row. There were five of us that were secretaries, and she was the receptionist, Each time she got pregnant, we all held our breath, hoping upon all hope, that she would carry this baby to term. She never did have her baby. She was so pretty, so kind. One day, she just cried and cried at work. She had helped plan baby showers for other women. I still remember the sleepers, booties, and rattle she bought for me as a gift when my first baby was born over 25 years ago. She bought blue — she just knew I was carrying a boy. We all laughed so much when I had a genuine little girl. As this young lady was crying on this particular day, she simply said, "I am wishing. Just wishing that I was pregnant again and that everything would be okay." A backwards longing. Wishing to be pregnant again. Knowing that she never would be. And battling grief as it appeared again and again. Just when she would get moving on in life, feeling better, she would take a look backwards and wish. Just wish. How this young lady suffered, and how hard she tried! Grief just would not let go of its tight grip on her heart. Not where child loss was concerned.

My aunt's sister had a baby that was born with something terribly wrong. The baby, a little girl, would never develop beyond the infancy stage. Every Friday evening our families would get together, make pizza, and watch a show on TV or listen to the radio. As a kid I was intrigued with this baby that never grew. She never cried either. She was always wrapped in a pink blanket with a little bonnet. While we all played and ate this baby stayed quietly in a bedroom. I remember so well the day we got the news that she died. I was so upset because I knew her brothers and sisters. We all went to school together. And, I knew that little baby. She came to my house every week.

After the funeral a lot of people came to our house and I remember the mother talking on and on about this little girl. She cried and cried and kept saying, "I always wanted her to grow. I wanted her to go to school with her brothers and sisters. I wanted her to run and play." It wasn't long until this family stopped visiting us. My aunt said that her sister went "crazy" — a term so often used for depression 50 years ago. I am sure that this mother's grief just overtook her. She longed for a healthy child. She accepted the fact that her little girl died. She knew that she had severe health problems from birth. But she just wished this had not happened. 1 really believe that this mother would have been happy just to keep this baby as she was for many more years. A parent's love is that strong. Sometimes grief over the loss is even stronger. Grief just does not want to let go. Ever.

I think it was this coming and going of grief that finally overtook Mary Todd Lincoln and President Lincoln when their son William died. They had already lost a four-year-old son, Edward. And they lost their beloved Thomas, affectionately known as Tad, when he became ill at age 18. But William had been the sickly one. He had so many other problems. History books tell us that the Lincolns worried so about William. He was so frail. Always susceptible to the cold. Always on the brink of pneumonia. When they looked back on their lives, the grief became almost unbearable. They had so many shattered dreams. Death lingered in their hearts. They wished for their sons. They wished William had not always been so sickly. Yes. They had come to terms with the deaths. Finally. Yes. They understood that people cared; they just did not always understand. Yes. They went through the initial shock period. Yes. Their lives finally began to see the sun shining through the clouds.

Death's final blow, the death of Abraham Lincoln, threw Mary Todd Lincoln over the edge. All of the past grief of her children's deaths resurfaced, and she finally spent a year in a sanitarium. She just wished things had been so different. Life would have been so very different with her sons and her husband. But, it was not to be. And looking back only caused the grief to grow. Child loss is not an easy loss to bear.

My friend Doug Lawyer said that he still has moments of looking back, wishing he had his little son. Certain songs, certain words, special places, trigger fond memories of that special little boy. Doug said that his heart grows heavy and he finds himself openly weeping. There seems to be a continuous tugging at the heart, a longing that things could have been different. What would Dougie be doing now? Would he be a gospel preacher like his daddy? Would he have a family of his own? Would he be living in Texas or Arkansas? I can just see Doug smiling through his tears as grief strikes his heart once again. Grief comes and goes, and seems to return at the most unexpected moments. Grief never is really a welcome friend.

One mother that I knew lost her son several years ago, and she has had a terribly difficult time adjusting to his death. He was killed so unexpectedly in a car accident very shortly before his high school graduation. It was a freak accident, one that never should have happened. It certainly should not have resulted in death. Yet it did. This mother went through an extremely difficult year of sadness and adjustments. Her son just was not supposed to die. Her husband grew bitter at the world and at God, and their marriage grew cold. It has been over 15 years now since this young man's death, and there still are days when this mother said she looks back in time and wishes that this had never happened. Grief still comes from behind and overcomes her. I talked to her just before Christmas, and she still cannot talk without crying. Her son's death seems to have served no real purpose. It has just left a void, broken hearts, and a lot of sadness. This mother is busy. She has the outward appearance of someone who is truly happy until . . . until her son's name comes up. She just wishes this accident had never happened. She wishes she still had her son.

I cannot help but find myself in a mixed-up turmoil over the devastation of child loss. There is nothing nice or right about it. It seems to leave a lingering hurt like nothing else. It seems totally out of kilter with God's ways and God's love. Many, many wonderful Christian parents have lost children. So many children suffer so terribly before they die. We are often left with such anguish.

And we have nothing real except questions — lots of questions and lots of pain. Child loss clouds and confuses our thinking. Child loss leaves us empty. There is no getting around it, child loss hurts for a very long time. For most of us the pain never really goes completely away.

In reading the account of the death of little Patrick Kennedy, I found myself totally absorbed in grief for this family. They had already lost two children by miscarriage. Their other two children were difficult deliveries resulting in Cesarean sections. One of these children was born so prematurely that he almost died. Now Patrick. Every precaution imaginable was taken to save little Patrick. But plans and preparation were not enough. He was born too soon, and he did not live. It was a time of extreme personal grief for the president and Mrs. Kennedy. Even the news media backed off and allowed the president time alone to weep. When the reporters saw his puffed, red face, tears falling from his eyes, that awful look of pain, they anguished with this father. Babies, so precious, so wanted, so pure, are just not supposed to die. And, yet they do. They die every day. The Kennedys had many, many moments of looking back and remembering. They fully understood what had happened. Three children had died. But, there were still many, many sad moments of wishing they still had their children. Wishing, but knowing it would never be.

Barbara Bush tells one of the most touching stories I have ever read about this backward longing for a child. In her book *A Memoir* she tells of a letter that her husband had written several years after their daughter Robin died. George Bush wrote this letter to his "Mum," baring his soul for the longing he still had for his little girl. He was blessed with four sons, but in his letter he wrote how something so special was missing. They needed a dollhouse amongst the forts. They needed a legitimate Christmas angel. They needed hugs that were a little less wiggly. They needed a girl. They had one once. And you can feel the heartache as his letter closes with a special longing for that little girl. His little Robin.

Was George Bush a weak man, unable to cope? Absolutely not. Was he a man who grew bitter over the death of a beautiful little daughter? Not at all. He was a father. And grief will always hold a stronghold in the corner of his heart.

I received a letter from a mother deep in grief. It has been exactly one year now since her loss. I had written her a letter to say that I remembered and I cared. I also wrote her about how much God cares, and sent her some Scriptures that I thought may be helpful. The letter I received in return seized my heart, and will not let go. I hurt so much for this family! In the letter, this mother explained that her relationship with her husband is about over. She said that she cries more now than ever before. She also explained how she also has not told her family of her intense grief. She does not think that they would understand. Then came the words that really got to me. "As far as God, I guess He cares. Right now I just can't get too excited about Him."

This woman is suffering so silently. So is her husband. They feel so alone. They are hurting so badly. As I talked to her later on, I understood completely what she was talking about. Life has continued on for everyone — her family, her friends, even her church family. Her relationship with her husband has been broken. They live in the same house, but barely even talk. I asked her what I could do to help. She cried and cried as she simply said, "Nothing. There is nothing that anyone can do. I just wish this had all never happened. I wish things were back the way they used to be."

She fully understands her loss. She has cried bitter tears over this loss. She has now gone back to work, but . . . she still wishes she had her child.

Is this mother being swallowed up in self-pity? No! Is she holding on to the past too long? Not at all. Is she a terrible person for asking questions of God? The psalmist David asked questions. Plenty of them. Job, a true man of God, sure had questions. God never called them terrible. Grief has just resurfaced and does not seem to want to go away for this woman. It hits her at odd moments. And she feels so very alone. So very lost. She is left wishing that her life had just been left alone. She was so happy before. Why this? Why now? Why at all? Grief brings with it a sadness that so often leaves us longing for what used to be.

The Inspirational Writings of Catherine Marshall is a book that is a true boost to one's faith. Catherine Marshall writes with such clarity, such simplicity, and such relevance. Catherine devoted a lot of her writing to the adjustments she had to make when her husband, her beloved Peter, died. Later on in her writing, though, Catherine talks about another loss, the loss of a young baby girl, her first granddaughter. Amy Catherine was born genetically damaged in her lungs, kidneys, and brain. Doctors at Children's Hospital in Boston offered no hope.

Friends and loved ones from all around the country gathered to pray for little Amy's healing. God did answer the prayers, but not in the way Catherine and all the others expected. Amy Catherine died.

Catherine Marshall was desolate for months. "What went wrong?" she wept. She was overtaken by grief, and for several months this woman of such grand faith was shaken. Visibly shaken. She searched for answers. She longed for this little girl. Her son and daughter-in-law suffered tremendously. It was some 12 years later when Catherine Marshall finally was able to say that healing had taken place. Not in Amy Catherine, but in others. Eventually she said she saw that nothing went wrong. God is a sovereign God who overwhelms us with blessings, but retains the decisions about "times and seasons" in His hands. Her journal entries indicate that grief surfaced and resurfaced throughout the years for Catherine Marshall over this loss. She certainly was not a woman of weak, doubting faith. She was a woman who wanted her beautiful granddaughter to live. She longed for something that just could not be. And it took a long, long time to get beyond this. 1 am not sure if she ever totally erased this longing from her life. Grief runs that deep and lives in the heart that long.

In talking with countless parents who have lost children, there seems to be one central thread that connects all of those who have suffered this particular grief and loss. Every one of the parents that I have talked with, no matter how many years had passed since the death, no matter how old the child was, no matter what the reason for death, I cannot think of one parent that said they were totally satisfied with the way this tragedy had happened. Many said they felt they had become more sensitive to others. Many were able to go on in life and accomplish great things. Many seemed adjusted and even peaceful. But not one that I talked with was able to say, "I'm glad that it happened." Everyone seemed to have a small, lingering sadness that quietly whispered, "I still wish I had my child."

One particularly sweet couple especially comes to mind as I think about this. This couple went through college, got well-established jobs, and were fine Christians. They were now ready to begin a family, and they were blessed with a pregnancy right away. The pregnancy was wonderful, the birth glorious, and they had a beautiful, blue-eyed blonde daughter. She was so pretty! When this beautiful little girl was six months old, the parents noticed her eyes did not seem to follow objects, and she did not seem to have responses to noise. They had her checked, and initially they were told that all was well. After two more months, physical development did not seem to be normal. Now there was cause for concern. This beautiful little girl had an extremely rare genetic disease, and she would inevitably die. This young couple suffered like none I have ever known. They literally watched helplessly for four years while their beautiful little girl wasted away. She grew some, but never could walk. She always remained in diapers. She was totally deaf and blind. She finally was unable to swallow, and it was a painful, dreadful death for this sweet, little girl and for her parents.

This couple did not grow angry at God, but they did search for answers in their grief. They eventually had three more children — all healthy, I am thankful to say. They will tell you they appreciate life so much more because of this little girl's death. They will tell you their children are a constant source of blessing to them. They remained extremely close as a husband and wife. But grief still overcomes them, although it has been almost 15 years now. Every time a family picture is taken. Every time they pack for a vacation. Every time they see a little blue-eyed blonde smile at them, their heart aches until it feels like they will just break. They are happy people today, but they still look back from time to time, and just wish they had their first-born child. They just wish things were different. They really wish they had that little girl. Only then would their family seem complete. Only then would they feel whole. Only then would they stop hurting. If they only had their sweet little girl.

What about parents that have no long-term memories of a child? What about parents that lost children early in a pregnancy? They had no time to get to know their child. They have no real reminders, only dreams shared between themselves. Dreams of the future, of what might have been.

In reading of so many accounts of early child loss, I was especially touched by what was discussed in the book *A Silent Sorrow*. Scores of parents were counseled and talked with after the early loss of a child during pregnancy. The grief seems to be strong, casts a lingering shadow, and tugs at the heart just the same as in a later child loss. This is just now beginning to be recognized. For years parents suffered early pregnancy losses so silently. As parents remember, as they look back with a tender yearning for what might have been, they hurt. They do not have memories of happy moments spent together. They do not have a person to talk about with others. But they did have a child. For a brief moment. Their child. They shared a joy beyond belief. An anticipation of wonderful days and years to come. And then, everything just ended so abruptly. Probably the most difficult part about early child loss is that it was so early. The child held no real meaning to anyone except you. No one understands your sadness, your tears, your longing for what may have been. Others forget; you do not. This is probably one reason why early pregnancy loss is so silent. The grief continues to come and go for these parents, and people do not even begin to understand.

One father recounted two early miscarriages that he and his wife endured. Shattered dreams. Disappointment. A longing to hold a little baby. Then they were blessed with a son. A healthy, wonderful son. They longed for another child and several years later they were blessed with a pregnancy. They watched the beating heart on the sonogram monitor. A beautiful, exciting sight! They were extremely cautious during this pregnancy, and the doctor was so very sensitive to their needs. He said they could come into the office any time just to listen to their baby's heart beating.

Two days later, they had a small gathering for their son's birthday. Nothing fancy — a cake and a few friends. They wanted no additional stress to interfere with this pregnancy. This mother went to use the bathroom, and much to her horror, she was bleeding. Within two hours she was hemorrhaging. The next day at the doctor's office was a total nightmare. There was no more baby. The little heart that was beating so beautifully just hours before, was no more. Hopes and dreams were gone. The father said he was "empty." The mother could not even talk. They have gone through years of ups and downs in their grief. No one seems to understand this couple. Friends often say, "You have one healthy child. What more could you ask for?"

They have fully accepted what happened. They know they

lost three children, and they have one precious son. So, what is the problem? Why do they have continued bouts with grief? They just wish sometimes that things had worked out differently. Grief still shares a corner of their hearts, and probably always will. The grief is not as bad as it used to be. But every now and then it hits. There is a longing for what may have been. That is just how grief is. That is exactly how child loss is.

For parents who have the lingering pain of a missing child, this backward longing in their grief can be the most difficult aspect of all to deal with. So much guilt is associated with a missing child. There is probably never a day that is not touched with a genuine longing for what might have been. If only I had not left my child alone for that short while. If only I had not allowed her to walk alone to her friend's house. If only I had been watching the yard. If . . . if. . . . Things would just be so different. There are a million ifs that cloud the mind and cause additional grief.

Along with this agony comes the pain of wishing. I just wish none of this had ever happened. I didn't ask for this pain. I loved my child so much. I want to see my child, to touch my child again. I just wish. . . .

How does a parent who has a missing child stop looking back? In their backward look, they had a child. The present has left them without a child. And the future only has questions. I wonder if I will ever see my child again. The agony of having a missing child for even a few hours can seem like an eternity.

To go day after day, week after week, year after year, is almost incomprehensible. Grief wraps the heart with a tight cord that pulls us right into the future. It is so hard to not look back in this type of loss, and just want to make the past a permanent retreat. The present just hurts too much. And the future is too unknown. My heart aches in such a special way for parents who have missing children. It would be so difficult to go on, and yet we must. We know it. We simply must.

Parents who have lost older children have somewhat of a mixed blessing with having had many years with their child. They have that thing called "memories." Memories can often serve a useful purpose in child loss. Not one parent alive has only fond, wonderful memories of a child. We all have some rough spells with our children. Many children have gone through difficult years, leaving behind a difficult legacy. But in this looking back a parent has the ability to sift through the mind-full of memories and filter out the bad ones. Quite often when an older adult child dies, parents have had the blessing of time together with their child. Time to mend any conflicts. Time to draw closer to each other. Time to become friends. A backward longing in grief can sometimes offer a small bit of solace when a parent is flooded with fond memories. These memories can be similar to making deposits in a bank. When you feel so alone, so depleted, so empty, you can pull out a memory that will help bring a wistful smile to your heart. Yes. You long for your child. You wish your child did not have to die. You still just wish this never had to happen. But years with your child has allowed you something very precious that not all parents have — time. And time with a child gives you that wonderful blessing of fond remembrances.

In your grief, in your longing, in your looking back, allow your precious memories to offer some comfort, if only just for the moment. Allow your heart to be warmed by these memories. Perhaps when grief swells up and wants to overcome you, your memories can be a comfort. Memories helped my grandmother so much. She lost two of her three adult children in less than one month. I truly believe that her memories, her looking back, her thinking of special times with her children are the only things that helped pull her through the tidal waves of such deep returning grief. Yes, she still wished she had her children. But in her case, her many years together with them helped her in her grief. At least her memories helped for the moment.

My grandfather, by the world's standards, was not an educated man. In fact, he only received a couple of years of formal schooling. And he never did learn to write his name. That always stunned me. As a little kid I tried and tried to teach him to write his name, but he never did learn.

He signed his paychecks from the saw mill with an X. But one thing stands out in my mind about my grandfather. He had a no-nonsense, practical approach to life. He was not a great spiritual man. In fact, he knew very little of God — only Bible stories that had been passed down to him. But he knew hardship. He knew sorrow. He knew death. He was not a daydreamer. He knew that life was as difficult as the stormy seas that rolled in to shore. He also knew that somehow you had to continue to live through the storms.

As a young girl, I was a great wisher, always clinging to the old Sears Roebuck catalog. I always wished we weren't so poor. I wished for a certain dress. Just always wishing. My grandfather would always say, "You can wish all you want, but it won't change what is." He said it with a smile, but he always reminded me that wishing for things to be different never changed anything. As harsh as this sounds, as cruel as it seems, it is true. And this one truth has helped me through many difficult hours. We can be overcome by a longing for what is not. This is especially true in the area of child loss. Or we can have momentary minutes of looking back, wishful thinking — even temporary wishing — but knowing ultimately that this is not how things really are. Child loss has occurred. That is such a difficult thing to face, especially when we are wrought with grief. We do have choices though. We can choose to pause and look back for a moment, and we can choose, we must choose, not to get stuck in our backward longing. It serves no real purpose except to add to our burdens and multiply our grief.

How can a husband and wife put back together broken dreams, push aside the feelings of guilt that often accompany child loss, and comfort the heavy hearts that never totally mend? It is not an easy thing to go on after you lose a child. In fact, it is an incredibly difficult thing to fight the returning waves of grief that often overpower us. It takes a husband and wife working together, holding onto one another, helping each other through the pain. Hopefully, when one is overcome with grief, the other one can help. That is what helped George and Barbara Bush to survive the bitter hours of grief. They learned to lean on each other, gaining new strength from one another.

Brief moments of looking backward are quite normal. It helps for couples to share their grief, their longings, their shattered dreams together. It is necessary for a couple to share this part of grief together, for it is the sharing of these intimate moments that will eventually bring a couple closer together in their hour of pain. When a couple can share this backward longing together, they can help each other to survive the throbbing pain of grief. Maybe this is what made it so difficult for Jackie Kennedy and Mary Todd Lincoln in their child loss. Somehow, their husbands had such a difficult time sharing this part of grief with their wives. They grieved. They grieved bitterly. They had the longings that are so natural in child loss. They just wished that this had never happened. But these couples did not always share in their grief. This made is so much more difficult for them to bear.

As I was writing this book, I knew that it would not be easy to talk with many parents who have suffered with child loss. I also knew that I would be opening up some wounds of my own that had not closed. But more than anything, I knew that I wanted to help, and it has been my prayer that this book will be a way of allowing me to tenderly touch many parents struggling with all of the sadness, the loneliness, the questions, the longings, for their child. The irony of this all is that quite unexpectedly I became pregnant. A new life. A blessing that I felt I did not really deserve. A blessing that I cherished. I was afraid. I was astonished. I was thrilled. As the weeks moved on, I was falling crazy in love with this baby. It was strange writing about loss while I was experiencing new life. I was so much more aware of the blessing of life. And then just when I was begging to feel comfortable with this new life, with this baby, this love shared between my husband and me, it happened. Only it was different this time. The bleeding started and stopped, almost like I was being teased. My body remained pregnant; tests confirmed a baby. Maybe the baby would continue to grow. Maybe. Hopefully. Prayerfully. But no. Slowly, almost with a torture, my uterus contracted. It pained. It stopped. It started. My body seemed to be playing games with me for several days. Then finally on a Thursday evening at 11:30 I delivered my baby at home. Developed tissue to some; a baby to me. I held what was not to be in my hands and I wept. This little life so real, so wanted, so loved, would not continue on. Bitter tears fell as the remains of this baby were washed away. A cruel joke. I did not ask for this to happen. I did not need it to happen. Not now. But it did, and my heart was once again pierced, and I will always remember. A part of me will always wish that I could have had this baby.

Why did this happen? I do not know. Why during this particular time? I do not know that either. Did God have a particular purpose for allowing this, or did Satan think it would be a good time to have me feel real pain again? I do not know. This one thing I do know. It hurt terribly to lose this child. My husband and I must once again feel the pain of losing a little one. And it just plain hurts. And, oh, I wish it had not happened! I really wish this baby would have continued on and could have come to be a part of our family. But the sad fact is that the baby died. We will never hold this child. And that really hurts.

As my husband and I struggle with this loss, we know enough about child loss to know that we both are deeply hurting. And we know that it is easier to hurt together. We know we still love God. We do not believe that He took this baby from us in order to pain us more, or to hurt us. We know all of this and yet . . . as we spoke again this evening while washing the dishes, I knew. I knew that we will always hurt over this loss. We talked of growing old together and how we will long for the children that we lost. This baby would have been such a joy to all of us. Grief will always be a step ahead, a step behind, and in the corner. Always. Child loss is just that way.

Because child loss is such a delicate loss, it deserves extraordinarily tender care. Lifelong care. It is so important for a husband and wife to hold onto each other, especially during the times when there is that backward longing. That longing for what was, but what you know can never be. Far too often we hide our feelings from each other and pretend that all is okay. One of my daughters was talking to me the other day and she said, "I really don't worry about you as much as I do Dad. You always tell us how you feel. We never know about Dad." She was right. Dads are generally more quiet. But they don't hurt any less. I can assure you of that. Wives, draw close to your husbands. Hurt together. Do not allow quietness to be mistaken for lack of understanding or lack of hurting. Husbands, be patient. You wife has extra emotions to deal with. Her body actually housed this child that you shared. It is an experience that cannot be put into words completely. I still grope for words to explain how it feels to nurture a baby. All I know is that it is an incredibly fascinating feeling. A God-given process. A blessing beyond belief. To lose a child is to lose all of that and more. To lose a child is to lose love. That hurts. When grief comes back on the rebound, talk together about it. That helps so much. Some of my greatest comfort has come from talking with my husband about our shared sorrows. The pain is so much easier when it is shared.

When you are all alone in your sorrow, and we all face aloneness at some of the most difficult times of child loss, turn to God. So many times it feels like God is a million miles away.

So distant. He is not far away. Remember that He is near. He promises that. He tells us that over and over again in His Word. The only time He is distant is when we push Him away. In your lonely longing, turn to Him. He cares. "The Lord is good; His lovingkindness is everlasting, and his faithfulness to all generations" (Ps. 100:5). Our Lord knew sorrow. He sorrows with us. "Jesus wept" (John 11:35). If we cast our burdens on Him, our load will be lighter. "Cast your burden upon the Lord and He will sustain you" (Ps. 55:22). When the way seems so lonely and the road seems to rough, allow Him to carry you. "In my trouble I cried to the Lord, and He answered me" (Ps. 120:1). In your longing, remember that as a child of God there will be a day when you will know no more tears and no more sorrow. "And He shall wipe away every tear from their eyes; and there shall no longer be any death; there shall no longer be any mourning, or crying, or pain; the first things have passed away" (Rev. 21:4). And in our weakness, we can become strong. "For when I am weak, then I am strong" (1 Cor. 12:10).

Hold on. There is help. There is hope. There is peace. With God, there is life. Yes. Even in child loss there is hope and life. Especially in child loss there is hope and life. Death is not the end!

Chapter 8

"I Can Feel!"

Most people who have suffered the pain of child loss describe the loss as being similar to a temporary state of having no feeling. You may go through all of the daily motions of life, but without really feeling a thing. Numb. Numb to the world. Numb to everyone around you. Numb to anything good. Numb to anything bad. There is a period of time when there seems to be absolutely no feeling.

This absence of feeling appears at different times for every person who has suffered child loss. When talking with a mother who had lost her young daughter to leukemia, I told her I was attempting to put together this book and I would really appreciate any insights she could give me. I said it would be especially helpful if she could tell me when she actually felt like life took on meaning again. I wanted to know when she actually felt like truthfully saying, "I can feel!" I was not expecting the reaction that I got from this young mother.

She became quite upset with me. "How can you even ask such a question? This is too difficult a question. Beginning to feel again is so very different for everyone. Child loss does not follow any special formula!"

After she settled down, we did talk for quite a while. This young mother had experienced a very slow walk back to life after her daughter died. It was not easy for her at all. She slumped into a deep depression for almost two years, and her feeling for life came back very slowly, day by day. Sometimes hour by hour. There was no one specific event, no one special moment that made her want to feel like enjoying life again.

As we talked, her hands trembled and she cried very softly. She has gone back to teaching school. She exercises every day. She is even taking night classes to broaden her education. She is active in her community. She has gone back to church. She can now look at a young child and see beauty in that little one without feeling bitterness or jealousy. She can now feel. However, what she feels is not quite the same as she felt before. Keep that thought in mind, as this will be discussed at length later in this book.

When I was 11 years old, my mother contracted a bad case of the measles. She was 30 years old, and had always been a picture of good health. We lived on a big chicken farm, and she was used to putting in long, hard hours of work each day. When she realized she had measles, she did not feel like losing a week of work, so she called the doctor. He made a home visit, which was the norm for those days. He confirmed the measles and said he would give her a shot of penicillin which was the new wonder drug of that day. She insisted on a "double shot." She just did not have time to be sick. The doctor complied with her wishes, and he was on his way.

By late evening the fever was going down, but a terrible rash was developing all over my mother. Between the measles and the new rash, she looked a mess. She went to bed early, and said she would be fine in the morning. I will never forget the nightmare of the following day, for it changed the course of her life forever. She let out a scream, "Help me! I can't move!" I went running to her and found her red and swollen. But even worse, her legs were paralyzed.

By noon she was carried away in an ambulance, struggling for the next 45 days for her very life. When she returned home, it was with a walker and the solemn words that she would never walk alone again. She had an allergic reaction to the penicillin and had severe damage to her nerve endings. To make matters even worse, she now had no feeling. Totally numb. Her feet felt like two blocks of wood. She could not begin to feel where those two blocks of wood tried to take her.

After a little more than a year had passed, one morning I heard another scream. "I can feel! Come here quick. I can feel!"

Little prickly sensations were coming back to my mother's legs and feet. She had me prick her several times with a pin, then run a popsicle stick across the bottoms of her feet. And she was right. She could feel — even if it was only a small amount of feeling. My mother never did get beyond the pins and needles stage of regaining her feeling, but it was enough feeling to allow her to learn to walk again without the aid of the walker. She always wobbled. Her balance was somewhat off. But she could walk! An incredible feat! And she could feel. That was the most wonderful thing of all.

Thankfully, my mother did not know then that she would lose all feeling once again in four years. Only this time, it would be her heart that would be affected. When my 13-year-old sister died, my mother's heart went numb. It was a long, long time until she regained enough feeling back to really say, "I can feel." And just as with her legs and feet, her heart never got beyond the pins and needles stage of feeling. Her heart remained somewhat off balance. And many of her days were difficult. Child loss just wounded her heart right to the nerve endings, and it was so very difficult to regain back that feeling she once had for life.

The intensity and length of time of numbness is unique to each and every parent that loses a child. That gentle awakening may take months, and in some cases even years, to finally occur. A broken heart is not an easy thing to mend.

A lengthy story of child loss was recently told to me by a professional health care worker. She had been so impressed by this family that she just had to tell me of the particular events. As the story was told, there was a mother who had four young children and was pregnant with the fifth child. She began to notice some problems with her oldest child. At first she and her husband thought the problems were behavioral due to another baby on the way. But the problems were much deeper than that. The little girl had a very rare genetic disease which would result in an early death. This mother and her family cared for the ill child at home for several years. She expressed to others how the family became a stronger, more solid unit because of having to care strenuously each day for this child who was reduced to a vegetative state. The little girl lived much longer than expected. Eleven years, to be exact.

Then, the words that followed really got my attention. The

mother said that never once did she question God. Never once did she blame God. Instead, she focused on the cross of Jesus. I was left with such mixed feelings after hearing this. This most certainly is the type of faith that we all long for. It is the type of genuine strength we strive for and we hope to attain. But the harsh reality is that for most of us, even those with an intense love of God, we do not have such solid, positive experiences during the loss of a child. These feelings and understandings may come several years after the loss, but very rarely do they come at the time of the child's death. There is almost always intense pain. And with that pain there usually is a period of numbness. A time when you just cannot seem to muster up the energy or the understanding to enjoy life. You just do not feel the same about anyone or anything any more.

It is quite normal to feel hurt, cheated, drained, depleted, and devoid after experiencing the loss of your child. Why do I even mention this episode of child loss? Because I have talked to so many parents who have lost children who go through so much agony, so much unnecessary guilt, because they cannot bury a child one day and get up and shout for joy the next day. I was so happy to hear of this mother's account of her solid, immovable faith.

But I also was greatly reminded that not all people can endure the pain of child loss like this. Does that mean they have no faith? Certainly not. A broken heart, yes. But I would not dare to tread the line of pointing a finger at someone's faith because they need the precious gift of time to gain back the sense of feeling life once again. Most people need a great deal of time to gain back a sense of balance, perspective, and feeling into their lives.

Especially after a trauma so numbing as child loss. I believe God allows us the gift of time. We should not be too harsh on ourselves if we cannot wake up two weeks after the loss of our child and "snap right out of it." Give yourself the gift of guilt-free time. Feeling for life will come back to you. Just when that feeling will return is uniquely personal. But you will one day be able to say, "I can feel!" You can be assured of that. Just give yourself time.

Some friends of mine just recently lost a young adult son to cancer. He fought a good fight, but conventional cancer treatments did not work; neither did the experimental treatments. This family is a strong Christian family, and they were real heroes to many people during the months of their son's suffering. They were so brave. They were so trusting. They were so accepting.

Two weeks after the death of this young man, strange things began happening. These parents had real questions to ask God. Why their son? Why at this particular time in his life? So many cruel people of the world seem to go on and on, and even prosper while sowing bad seeds. This young man was a devoted Christian. Why did he have to die?

These parents are also going through a real pulling away spell. They do not want to see or hear from anyone. They feel so alone in their grief, so isolated. So betrayed. Yes. Even betrayed somewhat by God.

They also said that they feel totally numb. Here is that word again. Numb. Devoid of all feeling. Life has lost all meaning. They appear to have lost purpose and direction. They just cannot gather the strength to get things back together again. They are devastated because they thought they were handling this whole thing so well. They think they are letting people down. They believe that their faith should be stronger.

My heart truly aches for this couple. They lost their only child. He was such a fine young man. Why shouldn't they feel sad? Why shouldn't they have some questions for God? Why shouldn't it take some time for the pain to subside? Why shouldn't they feel lost and just wandering for a while? These are all normal feelings. Yes. Even normal feelings for good, solid Christians. This couple needs the blessing of time to help them gain back some feeling for life. Their hearts have been numbed by such pain from losing their only child, Just as sure as the sun rises each new day, in time they will gain back the feeling of wanting to live life again. And they will live life with enthusiasm. It is just going to take some time. Broken hearts take time to heal. God knows and understands that. We need to be aware of that, too.

I was talking to a young man recently who has suffered some severe blows. His marriage of over 20 years is shaky. He has a lot of pressure to produce well at work. And on top of that, he lost a child. Through misted eyes he asked me if I had some sort of formula he could follow. Some rules or guidelines that would help him to feel better. He is hurting and just does not have much feeling or enthusiasm for life right now.

As I thought about this question, I realized once again that there is no formula, no set of rules to follow in child loss. How does one measure love and loss? How could anyone ever prescribe for you what only you feel? There is just enough uniqueness in child loss to make each loss distinctively different. Gaining back a sense of feeling — a love of life — is totally unique to each parent. Even within the husband and wife relationship, feeling for life will come back at different, unexpected times.

Several months ago I received a letter from a mother who had lost her adult son quite unexpectedly. He died instantly of a massive heart attack. This woman went on to explain how she got through her son's death, how helpful friends were, and how meaningful God was to her. Then, about a year later, she became quite ill. After seeing her doctor, she was diagnosed as having depression and high blood pressure. She continued on in her story telling me how difficult that year was. She was forced to make a decision concerning her work. The bottom line was that she was going to have to pull up roots and move to another state if she wanted to keep her job. She still was struggling in her grief, and this move just seemed to make matters worse.

This mother had always loved people and loved life. She found herself to be negative with everything and everybody. She eventually lost all feeling for life. She went through the motions of the daily routines of life, but that was it. Nothing had much meaning. When her son died, so much of her life died, too. In despair she went to another physician. The doctor spent a great deal of time with this mother and eventually realized that her main problem was her grief. She no longer felt much of anything for anyone because she had lost so much purpose. So many dreams were shattered. Her son was gone and the days still seemed so long and lonely.

Through this doctor's gentle caring, amazing things began to happen to this mother. As she talked and cried, she unraveled so much pain that had been harbored inside. Within less than another year this mother was back to living and feeling. What was it that helped her so? What was her secret? What helped her get feeling back into her life?

As I corresponded with this mother, she explained that her coming back to life was a gradual awakening. She had many,

many days of fighting tears and depression. Then, gradually, ever so slowly, she noticed that she began to hear the birds sing. She was smiling as she took her daily walk. Sometimes an entire week passed with no crying. She even began to enjoy her new location, and made several new friends. She said that probably the single greatest factor that helped was time. Time. Time to allow her son's death to become real. Time to allow her heart to adjust to all of the changes. Time to see things as they really were. Time to understand that even in the midst of life's most cruel circumstances, life and love continue on. Beauty is all around us, and eventually — in time — that beauty will be seen again. And that is exactly how this mother came to say, "I can feel!" She needed the blessing of the balm of time.

Recently I had the privilege of meeting with a large group of counselors in preparation for this book. We discussed in depth all aspects of child loss. By far the most difficult thing for most parents seemed to be getting this "feeling" back for life again. Countless stories of child loss were related to me, and each story had its own intense pain, its own drama. What seemed so important to me was the fact that eventually parents do get back to living again after the loss of a child.

The feelings of joy and a love for life seem to come for most parents ever so gradually. Slowly but surely the day arrives when life seems happy again. I do not believe that anyone who has ever had a child die will be the same. How could they be? When a broken heart mends there is always a scar left behind. But, even with the scar it is possible to feel, really feel, again. I think that every parent who has lost a child needs that blessed assurance that one day it will be their turn to say, "I can feel!"

One particular story that the counselors told seemed to stay with me. A very humble family lost their only son. He was only seven years old when he died in a school bus accident. These parents had a tremendously difficult time coping with the loss of their only son. They left his room as it was: bed unmade, books on the floor, clothes in a pile in a corner of the bedroom. They left the door to their little boy's bedroom open so that every time they walked down the hallway they would see those reminders of their son.

Friends became alarmed several months after this little boy died. The father was like a robot. He seemed to mechanically go to work on cue. Then he would come home to a dark, dirty house where he found his weeping wife. A health care worker went to visit this family one day, and she was shocked at what she found. Dust was everywhere. Dirty dishes. Trash piled up. Clutter in every room. The little boy's room was perfectly intact since the day of his death. It was made to look somewhat like a shrine.

The lady that was visiting saw immediately that this couple had lost their ability to feel. In her caring and sensitivity, she asked if she could vacuum and dust the house. Then she asked if she could wash the dishes. After this was completed, she had a cup of tea with this young couple. In their talking, she realized the need for them to be able to say, "I can feel!"

Every week for several weeks the health care worker made brief visits to this home. Each week she would leave a small list of chores for this couple to complete. The first few weeks, only the dusting was accomplished. Over the course of six months, though, amazing things were happening. The work list grew larger by the couple's own choice. The visiting nurse helped them to get beyond the numbness left from their son's death to a point where they began to see purpose once again. Feeling was coming back, and it was like life being pumped back into them. There was nothing outstanding. There was nothing out of the ordinary that was done or said. There was no one thing that stands out in the couple's mind as being the spark that ignited them. Nothing. They simply needed the precious gifts of time and friendship.

I met a couple several years ago who had tragically lost their twelve-year-old son. He was the youngest of three boys, and he was everything any parent could ever ask for. Occasionally there will come along a model child. This young man happened to be just that. He was shy but strong in his basic moral beliefs. He was respectful yet assertive. He was obedient but innovative and creative in his thinking. He had begun his own business at the age of 10, and had made his first money investment by age 11. His parents were so very proud of their son. This particular young man won the heart of just about everyone that he met. He had a contagious smile and his eyes just seemed to sparkle with an excitement for all of life.

One morning on his way to school, a car was speeding, hit this young man's bicycle, and he was killed instantly. Gone. Just that quickly. Words cannot begin to describe the absolute horror, the crippling pain that this boy's family felt. On top of all of that, the community was paralyzed in its grief. Everyone knew this boy, and they loved him. His loss was felt by so many.

The mother of this young man is a very petite, soft-spoken lady. As she talked of her son, her eyes were moist, and her face became pale. She still missed him even though it had been nine years since his death. She said for the longest while she seemed to have lost all purpose in life. She just didn't feel like moving on. The bitter reality of her son's death had left such a dark, empty void in her life. She never thought that anything or anyone could even fill the tiniest part of that emptiness left by her son's death.

Getting excited about living was really the last thing on her mind, until. . . . She spoke so softly as she told me that one day she was crying and staring at her son's picture when she became fixed on his eyes. They reached out to her even in his physical absence. That's how a child's love is. This mother just held the picture and looked at her son for the longest while until something happened. Her cold, empty heart seemed warm. As she thought of her son she remembered how much he loved all of life. He loved people of all ages. He loved animals, especially horses. How could she go on like this and not love life, too?

That is how it happened for this mother. There was nothing spectacular that happened. Just looking at her son's picture and remembering his enthusiasm for life touched her heart. That was the beginning point for her. That was the beginning of her walk back to life once again. That was the beginning of her being able to feel.

I remember several years back after going through a particularly difficult miscarriage, I was feeling negative about everybody and anybody. I was so hurt, so disappointed. I felt so alone. Nothing much really mattered at that particular point in time. And, on top of that, nobody else seemed to feel the way that I did. As I listened to the daily conversations of people, they seemed so happy. Laughter seemed to fill everyone's heart except mine. At least that is how it felt to me at that particular moment.

One especially cold, dreary morning I was just sitting in a chair crying softly when my husband walked into the room. I must have looked as cold and dreary as the weather because he turned from me and began walking away. For some reason he stopped, though, and came back to me. He looked straight into my eyes and said, "Stop feeling so sorry for yourself. You are not the first person to ever lose a baby. And you will not be the last person to lose a baby. Look around you. Look at all that you have to remind you of life. It's time to get up and do something for someone." I was stunned! My ears were stinging. My husband had never talked to me that way before. He was cruel, and I got mad. How dare he!

I did stop crying and then I fumed. I replayed what he said to me that morning over and over in my mind. "Do something for someone." I think that is what got to me the most. I could not believe he would suggest such a thing. Not now. I was hurting and he knew that. Why did he say what he did? Why didn't he just hold me close and cry with me?

That day was a real turning point in my life. For some reason I have never forgotten those words spoken to me by my husband. In his wisdom and in his love for me, he knew exactly what would help me the most at this particular time. He knew how much I love people. All people. He also knew how much I love to do things for others. In my grief I had turned my pain and my thoughts inward. And that was okay to do. For a while that was okay to do. But I was stuck in a rut and I needed some gentle nudgings to get me out. Not everyone could have gotten away with talking to me like that during that time of loss. But my husband knew me better than anyone else, and he cared for me more than anyone else. He also deeply shared the same hurt of losing our child. A child that we wanted very much.

I reacted in just the way my husband knew I would. I got angry. In my anger, I decided to "show him a thing or two." I would do something for someone. And I did! I prepared a meal for a family that was going through an extremely difficult time with cancer. They were really suffering. I delivered the meal that evening, and I cannot begin to tell you what happened. My heart had feeling! I cried tears, but they were not all for me this time. I could sorrow with someone else. I could feel! Oh, it felt so very good to finally feel again!

I have never forgotten that particular moment. Memories of that single event have helped me through countless other painful circumstances. Later on, when I suffered even more painful losses than this miscarriage, I fell back on this experience to help me get through.

For me, doing something for someone else works every time. It helps me to focus my attention on someone else. Yes. My motivation at first was wrong. Anger. Anger is never a real good reason to do something. Yes. I had to really force myself to do something positive. I had to force myself to do something for someone else while I was hurting. But, there is something in that principle that really works. It helps to turn our thoughts away from self and to look outward. And it certainly helps to be able to honestly say, "I can feel!"

Let's try to pull all of this together and see what will really help you to be able to say "I can feel!" once again. This gradual awakening to the fact that life does go on in spite of our losses is probably one of the most challenging concepts to accept. When we hurt, we want others to hurt. When we have suffered a loss, we want others to feel some of that pain, too. This is especially true in child loss of any kind. We even become somewhat fearful to love again. We are so afraid. We are so afraid of being hurt and of having love snatched away again. And we somehow expect others to understand all of this and to be patient with us.

It is fine to be intensely sorrowful for a while. In fact, I would say that it is even quite healthy to express our deep sorrow over losing a child. It is also quite normal to feel numb to life all around you for a while. After all, a life — a precious life — was taken away, and that is not easy fact to accept. When your entire world has been turned inside out and upside-down, it takes a while to get back on level ground. And rightly so. What is not good for you or for anyone else is for you to stay in that deeply sorrowful state of mind and resist looking at life that is all around you.

As I talked with countless parents who have lost a child, one thing stood out in my mind as being a common thread to all. No one can do this for you. No one can force you to "feel" life again. No one can make you enjoy life, love life, live life, feel life again. Others can help get you to that point in your life, but the leap towards life must be made by you and you alone. I suppose this is basic to healing — taking responsibility. Being accountable for one's own self. At first I thought this idea sounded rather strong and severe. It almost seemed lacking in sensitivity.

But as I remember conversation after conversation with parents who were numbed by child loss, the same thing was true for each one. Each parent had to ultimately take that initial first step towards living again. For each and every parent that step comes at a different time and is marched to a different tune. But once the effort is made, the walk begins and the journey back to life becomes real.

This act of getting back to living again can be particularly burdensome for husbands and wives. We have already established the fact that men and women, moms and dads, grieve differently. Healing from the pain of child loss knows no timetable, nor does it follow any set of rules. For a husband and wife, knowledge of these facts can be crucial in maintaining a happy relationship. Many times men are somewhat forced back into the mainstream of living a bit sooner than women. This is probably due mostly to their jobs. A woman can also get away with showing her feelings more openly than a man. Even though a man may be forced to face work and the many stresses of the everyday work life soon after the loss of a child, he may show strength under pressure. The feeling of usefulness comes into full view.

That feeling of being needed is basic to anyone's healing response to life. All of us need to feel needed by someone. Husbands who have lost a child need to feel needed even more. They need to feel useful, appreciated, and unconditionally loved. Aren't these the very things that a child helps us to feel? Work can provide that avenue of doing something useful for a husband. Work can be a temporary way of filling the vast void left behind when that precious child died.

A wife will really travel a winding path trying to find a way to get to that point where she can say, "I can feel!" After all, even if a mother works a full-time job, her natural instincts most always kick in and motherhood still remains her top priority. Motherhood, not a job, makes a woman feel needed. Once a woman becomes a mother her objectives in life change. I believe that God made women that way. Do you see the difficulties these differences can cause between a husband and wife? A man will most likely throw himself into his work very shortly after the loss of a child. He may even excel like never before. He needs to fill an aching, empty spot. And he needs to be needed. A woman may withdraw for a period of time from work. She may even be encouraged to do so by her colleagues to help "get herself together." Her child was her main source of feeling needed. Everywhere she looks she sees empty reminders of how much of her life has been taken away. She sees the empty place at the table. She sees the empty bed and the toys resting quietly in the toy box. The washing machine no longer produces a hum with a load of grass-stained "best clothes." And her head no longer hurts from all of the background noise of incessant chatter from her little one. Her home is still, and so is her heart. And if her husband is busy working more hours to fill his hurting needs, who does she have? Who is there to help?

Couples need to work real hard in this area because the timetable for grief is so totally off balance. So is the timetable for getting back to living again. No two parents will begin to feel life again at exactly the same time, it just does not happen that way. Resentment, anger, and even jealousy can come onto the scene. One mother told me through clenched teeth that she was so jealous of her husband. She said, "It's just not fair! He doesn't hurt the way that I do!" I am solidly certain that no two hurts are ever quite the same. But that was not what made her jealous. She was jealous that he was beginning to see the possibilities for enjoying life once again. He was beginning to feel. He was beginning to smile again and it just did not seem fair.

So what are couples supposed to do? Suffer alone? Absolutely not. Go to another person for comfort? That surely will not strengthen a relationship. Should they live in separate worlds hoping to join forces someday? No. This is a marriage. A union. A lifetime commitment. Learn to be sensitive to the needs of each other always. Be sensitive to the needs of each other especially in child loss. If one is feeling better, do not feel guilty about that. Rather, gently point your mate towards life. Take a walk together, hand in hand. Talk together about your many blessings. Talk about the future. Dry each other's tears. And walk some more.

Smell a flower together. Or touch a snowflake. Watch a bird or a blade of grass. All of these things are small and seemingly insignificant, but they represent life. Life. Learning to look at the small things is often the beginning of one's passageway back to life.

Get away from the house together for a brief period of time.

Why? Because it is good to see people caught up in the everyday happenings of life. Even if it seems painful to you at first, get away for just a brief time. You will have fresh insights. Talk together. Share how you feel. A wife may not know that her husband is still struggling with pain from child loss unless he tells her. A husband may not understand why his wife cannot enjoy life yet unless she lets him inside her heart. The main thing is to "share your loss together." And be acutely aware that it is more likely than not that you will reach that moment of "I can feel" at different times. Be constantly understanding of the fact that this major step towards life is personal. It is so personal that each person must take that first step alone. But it is a most wonderful step to take. And once you begin your journey, each step will become just a bit more steady.

What about the mother or father who loses a child and is now alone? You have no mate to help you through the long, dark night. You have no one to dry your tears. You have no one to listen to your hurting heart. Who prods you on to living again? How do you find a way to feel needed? How do you keep from falling into a pit of lonely despair and just staying there? I am often reminded of the young mother I know who lost her little girl to a rare disease. Her marriage disintegrated shortly after the little girl died. She felt at odds with God for the longest while. She was numb, and she began to think she was going to stay that way. Life did not have much appeal at all.

One particular day she was totally drained from crying. It was well over a year since her daughter had died. Her husband had left several months ago. She felt like her life had lost all meaning. So she walked a lonely wooded trail and she cried. She sat on a rock and cried some more. Then she ran and she cried even more. As she was running she noticed an open field at the edge of the trail. She ran to the field and slumped down sobbing. As she cried she found herself calling out to God in her darkest hour. Talking to God was something she had not done in a long, long time. Through her tears she saw a tiny sparrow. The sparrow landed directly in front of her. She told me that at that point something happened to her. A verse from the Bible came to mind. "Look at the birds of the air, that they do not sow, neither do they reap, nor gather into barns, and yet your heavenly Father feeds them. Are you not worth much more than they?" (Matt. 6:26).

It was something so tiny and so ordinary that brought this mother to the point of wanting to feel again. A sparrow. A plain, ordinary sparrow served as a reminder of God's magnificent care and love. The time was right. It felt so good to "feel" again!

In your loneliest hour, during your worst times of despair, be assured that your are not alone. You are never alone. God has promised that He will see you through whatever pain you are called on to bear. Yes. He will even see you through the pain of child loss. "For He will give His angels charge concerning you, to guard you in all your ways" (Ps. 91:11).

Though others may not understand your loneliness and your tears, you have a God who does understand this blanket of grief that you are under. "Jesus wept" (John 11:35). When you think that you will never feel happy or complete again, remember God's faithfulness in carrying you through this lonely time. "The Lord sustains all who fall, and raises up all who are bowed down" (Ps. 145:14).

Keep reminding yourself often that God did not kill your child, rather He will help you get through this. "Thou hast taken hold of my right hand. With Thy counsel Thou wilt guide me, and afterward receive me to glory" (Ps. 73:23-24). And always, always remember who is in charge. You have a great and mighty God. A powerful God. An awesome God. He will not leave you — ever! "The Lord reigns; let the earth rejoice" (Ps. 97: 1).

As you close your weary, tear-stained eyes and meditate on God and His tremendous love and power, amazing things will begin to happen. Slowly but surely your eyes will begin to see beauty again. Your ears will begin to hear a new song. And your cold heart will begin to warm. You will feel! The earth will begin to feel alive again!

Chapter 9

The Sun Does Shine

Have you ever needed reassurance in your life that some day things would get better? There probably is not a person alive who has not struggled at some time in this area of living. We get so bogged down in our own problems that after a while we question whether or not life is all that it should be. We begin to wonder *Is anybody really happy?* Do these problems ever go away? Has anyone ever survived this pain of child loss and come out on top? We want to know answers to these questions. We *need* to know some answers to these questions. Does the sun really shine?

Eighteen years ago my husband and I asked that very question, "Does the sun really shine?" We asked that question quite literally. We were not sure about the sun anymore.

We had moved to a mountainous area in Pennsylvania where the elevation is quite high and the winters are quite long. If it is going to snow in the state of Pennsylvania, we can be sure that we will get the most snowfall. It is not unusual to have snowfall from mid-October to mid-April without much of a break in between. Along with a considerable amount of snowfall, there are usually very few sunny days. If you are a sun-loving person, this probably would not be a great place for you to move. The sun shines very little, and when it does, it is always a most welcome sight.

After a particularly long, bleak winter in 1978, my husband and I decided to do something really crazy. We took our income tax return check and bought plane tickets to Florida for the kids and us. That was back when plane fare was affordable for a family! Yes. We were going to Florida to see if the sun really does shine. What a memorable trip! We still talk about it today. We found out that the sun indeed does shine. And it shines gloriously! We left Pittsburgh airport in a foot of snow and we arrived in Daytona Beach in 81 degree temperatures. It was a warm, balmy February day in Florida. We felt like we had arrived in paradise.

We have never forgotten that trip of so many years ago because it made such a lasting impression. In fact, the phrase, "The sun really does shine," has become a favorite phrase in our home. When our weather becomes increasingly harsh and the sun has stayed hidden behind the clouds for several days, it is comforting to remember our trip. It is reassuring to know that somewhere in this world the sun is shining. And it is shining ever so brightly.

When we are going through a particularly difficult siege and we seem to have no let-up of problems, it is a great consolation to know that the sun will one day shine down on us again. That trip to Florida serves as a timeless reminder to us that somewhere behind those dark ominous clouds there is a sun still shining brightly. And one day it will be our turn again for the sun to shine on us.

What in the world does this all have to do with child loss? Actually, this basic concept has a lot to do with child loss. If we lose sight of the fact that life will get better — the sun does still shine — then we have lost a grip on one of the most important corners of life itself.

Losing a child is devastating. There is just no getting around the fact that any way you try to coin the phrase or soften the blow, the fact will still remain that your child has died. And that hurts. It hurts like no other pain that we know. Months after the death of a child every parent needs some sort of reassurance, some encouragement, something to hold on to that is a constant reminder that the sun does, indeed, still shine. Even in the midst of child loss, there can be smiles and joy. There must be smiles and joy because that is what life is all about.

You might be wondering just when this feeling that the sun does shine will come about. This is so very different for each parent that there can be no set of guidelines or rules laid out to follow. You will slowly gain back bits of sunshine in your life sometime after you begin to get a feeling for life again. You actually will catch yourself smiling occasionally but not really knowing why. That is the wonderful beginning of your emergence back into life.

A few months ago I received a lengthy handwritten letter from a mother whose son had died of a malignant tumor. This lady asked me to thank certain people for flowers, cards, letters, visits, and the like. She said, "I just don't think that I'll ever be up to thanking them myself. I just don't think I will ever feel good again." I was saddened by her letter until I read it over for the third time. Something caught my eye, and I knew at that moment that there would be a day when she would finally realize that the sun does still shine. This lady had designed her own letterhead on the computer. She had chosen ribbons and hearts — symbols to me of happiness and warmth. You see, life was beginning to take on new meaning for her and she didn't even realize it. This reassurance that there is a sun that still shines is a slow, gentle awakening to everything around you. In time, the sun will shine for every parent who has lost a child. The beams from the sun will shine just a little bit differently, a little deeper than before. But you will have that total assurance that the sun was shining all along. Allow yourself that most precious gift of time, and remind yourself often that the sun still does shine. One day you will awaken and you will actually feel its warmth all about you.

In the book *The Best of Catherine Marshall* an entire section is devoted to the dark period of time in Catherine's life following the death of her infant granddaughter, Amy Catherine. Catherine Marshall slumped into a period of withdrawal from everyone she loved, including her God. She battled despondency, and she finally succumbed to it. She had telltale dark circles under her eyes from lack of sleep. The sparkle in her lively eyes was gone. She just could not accept the face that God allowed precious Amy Catherine to die.

There had been prayer vigils. So many close friends were at the hospital praying. Catherine just knew that Amy Catherine would be healed. But, ultimately, she was not healed. In fact, beautiful little Amy Catherine died. This became Catherine

Marshall's darkest hour. She just did not understand. She no longer understood her God. She no longer trusted the power of healing and prayer. She no longer felt the presence of God in her life. As a result, she withdrew into a closed shell of despair and loneliness.

About six months after Amy Catherine's death, Catherine Marshall was still not moving ahead in her living. She was withdrawing from life. Her husband, Leonard LeSourd, became gravely concerned and decided to call together some of Catherine's best friends. They all loved Catherine and shared Leonard's concerns. They unanimously decided to confront Catherine about her lifeless condition.

Catherine, though deeply despondent, sensed the urgency in her husband's voice as he talked. She saw the anguish in the eyes of her friends when they said how anxious they were for her. Yet she could not respond with much of anything. Catherine had no feeling left. The sun was not shining where she could see or feel it. All was black. All was black until . . . in their course of talking, someone suggested that Catherine stop trying to understand.

That one very plain statement halted her thinking and she held on to that thought all through the night, Early the next morning Catherine was still thinking about that statement. Stop trying to understand. All along she had been pushing God and others for answers. She had been demanding answers to why Amy Catherine had to die. She simply must know the answer "why" or she could not make sense of life anymore.

As Catherine cried and thought more about her unhappiness and unrest, she finally realized what her friends had told her made a bit of sense. Sometimes there just are not answers. Questions concerning pain and suffering and death often just make no sense to us. Amy Catherine's death was one of those instances that left a big question mark. There was never going to be an appropriate answer. There never would be a satisfying answer. Child loss offers no real consolation, no real comfort. Children are not supposed to die. Pure, innocent, beautiful babies are never supposed to die. And yet they do. Why? We will never know the complete answer to that question. Never in this life.

It was at this point, this very moment of realization that there could be no solid answers to Amy Catherine's death, that

Catherine Marshall's life began to change. She explains this as being her turning point. Finally. Finally she could see a small beam of light in the cold, dark chambers of her heart. She absolutely knew that the sun was still shining. It had been shining all along.

Did Catherine Marshall walk right back into the light of life? Not at all. It took several more months for her to get back to where she could really see the sun shining in her own life and to feel love's warming rays once again. For her, the first initial step was restoring her broken relationship with God. She had been bitterly angry with God for not providing the answers to Amy Catherine's death. Once Catherine Marshall began to understand that there would be no answers, at least none that would satisfy her, she was able to once again go to God in prayer. She began the slow walk towards life, and ten of her most productive years of writing followed this period of dismay and darkness. Finally. Finally she was able to say that the sun does shine!

In talking with many different parents who lost children, one of the most troublesome areas for them to reconcile was this particular one — getting to the point of feeling like life is good again and staying that way. Not fluctuating back and forth between wanting to go on and not caring to move on. Every parent expressed to me that he or she wanted to get on with living at some point, but it was so hard to gather the energy to even think about going on for a long while. Guilt and jealousy seemed to take their toll, too.

One father told me how he still is battling jealousy. He lost his 22-year-old son. The son was an only child, and the father and son did everything together, including work. They had a carpentry business that they ran together. It is now almost two years since this man's son died from cancer and he said that he just cannot get to feeling right. He finds himself walking alone a lot. Walking and just thinking about what life could have been. Just thinking. He finds it almost unbearable yet to think of his son being gone. Forever gone. He is working only part-time because work is no longer a joy. It is a daily reminder of what used to be. He and his son had plans for the future. Big plans for a family business. They were going to hand the business down to the next generation. Now there would be no grandchildren either. This man said he gets consumed with jealousy when his friends talk about picnics, ball games, weddings, and the laughter of grandchildren. Just these words are bitter reminders of what was lost when his son died. He knows how he wants to feel. He knows that jealousy is not good for him. But the plain truth is that is how he feels right now.

As he was talking, his wife quietly smiled and said with calm assurance that she knows it is just going to take some more time. There is that all-important word again. Time. She said they both love children. They love people. They want to travel some. They just are having a tough time finding joy in other children and other people right now. Such a big chunk of that happiness is missing from their lives. They miss their son. You don't get over a lifetime of love in a few weeks. It just can't be done.

Child loss is no easy journey to complete. You have been pushed into a long, dark tunnel that you never wanted to enter in the first place. Now you must make that lonesome journey through the tunnel if you want to reach the light. Child loss is a rigorous journey, not a pleasure trip. Expect to take lots of falls before you reach the end of the tunnel. But be assured that there is warmth and light waiting for you. Keep forcing yourself to remember that the sun is still shining. Yes. The sun is still shining even on the bleakest day.

Some of you may be thinking how depressing this all is. This grief from child loss is so strong, so deep, so relentless. It seems that way, at first. In fact, it truly is that way for a long time. May I be so bold as to say that a parent who has lost a child will never be totally the same again? If you are expecting to feel joy in the same ways as you had before your child died, you have expectations that are too demanding of yourself. If you think that you will find joy in the same places as you did before your child died, you are putting undue pressure on yourself that is too great. When your child died, your life was changed. Forever changed. Allow yourself time to adjust to the injuries made to your heart.

Child loss causes dramatic changes. It will take several months for you to readjust your thinking to help you see life from a different angle. Remember Catherine Marshall? Some of her most productive years came after the death of Amy Catherine. Those years of productivity also came after a lengthy period of dark grief tinted with misunderstanding, guilt, and despondency.

I would briefly like to mention this idea of jealousy cropping up again. Not too many parents talk about it. Jealousy is a
difficult word to say. It is an even more difficult word to admit.
But I can assure you that jealousy fits into child loss just like a
missing piece of a puzzle. And if the jealousy is not dealt with at
this point it will only prolong the silence and the grief of child
loss.

When I miscarried the first time, I was devastated. I really
could not believe that this happened. Something else happened
to me, too. I began to feel something towards people that was
new to me. I felt jealous. A girl that I worked with, Linda, seemed
to have everything going for her. She had a great looking husband who adored her. She had a good paying job that she loved.
She was spoiled by her family, especially her dad. She lived in a
new home. And now she was pregnant. She was ecstatic. And,
you guessed it. Not only did her pregnancy go wonderfully well,
but she got her wish fulfilled. She and her husband had a beautiful, healthy baby boy. She had it all. Not really. But I perceived it
as being that way. I took the miscarriage issue and brought in
every possible problem that I was having, blew everything out
of proportion, and got even more despondent. On top of that, I
felt jealous. Even now I feel ashamed to say this. But child loss
does strange things to you.

In my mind, everyone's pregnancy went fantastically well.
Everyone delivered perfectly healthy children. Everyone else was
happy, except for me. Of course, this was not at all true, but I
was searching. I was trying to find answers. I was also trying to
find the blessed assurance that the sun would shine down on me
again. Instead I felt jealous. Added to that, I was burdened with
the guilt for feeling jealous. My nature is not to be a jealous
person. I really did not like "me" very much at all.

What helped? I kept extremely silent about this miscarriage.
Only a small handful of people knew that I had lost a baby. But
an older, wiser lady from church took an interest in me. She must
have sensed a sadness and she made a suggestion that impacted
me for my life. She suggested that I volunteer some time each
week with handicapped children. At first, I totally backed away
from this idea. Why would I want to anything like that? But Mollie
persisted. She kept asking me to be a volunteer.

Finally, and quite reluctantly, I decided to give this volunteer thing a try. The day I walked through the doors to that room-ful of children, my life was forever changed. My eyes filled with tears and my heart swelled with compassion. I had been so wrong in my thinking. Not every baby is born perfect and healthy. Mothers do have difficult deliveries that sometimes result in permanent health problems for the baby. Cystic fibrosis does exist. Cerebral palsy does afflict beautiful children. Children are born with chromosomal defects.

Oh, I was so ashamed of my thinking! It was time. The time had come for me to see beyond myself and look to the needs of others. I could feel! I felt so much love for these children — beautiful children. And it helped me so much to be able to see that the sun was still shining.

Yes. Even in the midst of child loss the sun was shining. It was time to allow the sun to shine. It was time.

In talking with an older mother who lost an adult daughter to cancer, she said that she had to fight a most difficult battle against jealousy and guilt. She began to dislike every mother who had a healthy daughter to call on the phone each day, to go shopping with, and to share secrets with. Her daughter had been a fun-loving, energetic young woman who was diagnosed with cancer. In six months this daughter was dead. Although her daughter was married and had a child, the mother and daughter relationship remained close.

I had not seen this family for at least 10 years, and have recently had the occasion to talk with them. It has taken this mother nearly 12 years to get beyond this jealousy and guilt, and to finally realize that the sun still does shine.

What finally helped her? The simple act of letting go. She finally had to just let go of the pain. She described it as letting go of a balloon and watching it sail off into the vast expanse of the sky, carrying her jealousy, guilt, and bitterness away. She had become so miserable in her grief that the sun had been blocked out of her life. One day while watching her grandchildren play, she said it finally dawned on her. Life was all around her. Beautiful, wonderful life. Her eyes had just been too clouded by tears to see the sun. But the fact is that the sun had been there shining all the while. The time just had not come yet for her to let the light shine in. And when the time arrived to let go, she breathed in the air and soaked up the life that surrounded her and it felt so good. It was so good to be alive.

Did she jump back into life right away? Not at all. It is taking her a long time to feel that sense of true joy once again. Does she still cry? Yes. I got a call a few weeks ago and she was going through a real distressful time. She was crying, but the tears were not jealous, guilty tears. They were more silent, more subdued. They were tears that knew life would never be quite the same again. They were tears that had the assurance that the sun was still shining. They were tears that said simply, "I really miss my daughter today. But I know that I will feel better tomorrow." They were more calm tears. More peaceful tears. They were tears flowing from a mom's eternal spring of love. And these tears were okay.

Tomorrow she will look to the sun. Even though she has tears today, she knows assuredly that in spite of those tears the sun still does shine.

My dear friend Doug Lawyer has been a constant source of encouragement in my life. Whenever I think of laughter, joy, peace, and love, I think of Doug. His face has a wrinkle here and there, his hair has become silver, and his walk is not quite as spry as it once was, but Doug's heart . . . what a heart! I asked Doug what helped him get beyond the dark grief of his little four-year-old Dougie's death. Doug smiled that famous smile of his. "My God has just been too good. Look at all that He surrounds me with each day."

I hope someday to have a perfect peace, a full assurance in my God like that. Doug knew that God did not single him out and take his precious little son. Doug knew that God would walk hand in hand with him through the immense pain of losing his only son. Doug knew that the sun was still shining in spite of so much darkness surrounding little Dougie's death.

Doug is rare. His immovable faith in a good God is even more precious and rare. I do not believe I personally know anyone who is as steadfast and sure in his God as Doug. And Doug has that priceless quality of thoroughly enjoying all people. Every person is a precious gem in his sight. That is part of Doug's ability to see the shining sun. His love of God is an anchor in the worst of storms, including child loss.

Hidden deep within every heart is this same type of genuine love. It is like a spark waiting to be ignited. You never know just what or who may touch your heart to release these feelings of love, but when it happens you will finally sense a calmness about you. You will smile a soft smile and you will see. You will see that the sun is still shining. It has been shining all along. Yes. Even in child loss the sun still does shine.

Let me take just a moment to address parents who have the lingering devastation of a missing child. This particular type of loss is one that produces a daily battle of emotion, spirit, and will. Because there can be no real solid closure brought to this type of loss, a parent struggles every day with the idea of either giving up or holding on to hope. It is not within my realm of thinking to even imagine what I would do. Knowing myself as I do, I probably would hold tightly to even the tiniest shred of hope, despite the facts that may point in another direction. What parent wants to give up hope that their child may still be alive? It is comforting, at least for a while, to grip firmly to the hope that one day your missing child may return. But, how do you return to some semblance of normal living? How do you get some feeling back for life? How do you finally compose your thoughts and emotions enough to say that you know the sun is still shining when every single day is shadowed with the clouds of despair?

I truly believe that there is hope even in this situation. At some point you will be faced with that most difficult, most trying decision of all. Do I choose life, or do I choose to stay forever hidden by the clouds? Words such as trust, peace, hope, and faith take on an entirely new meaning for parents who have a missing child. There will come a time when sheer exhaustion from the ongoing pain of your loss will push you through a new door. You will enter the room of trust. Trust that God will somehow take care of your child. Trust that somehow things will work out. Trust that prayer will offer peace from the turbulent storm of doubt and despair. You will realize that even though your life has been torn apart by this shocking experience of child loss, you can — you must — find some solace and rest. I firmly believe that such parents develop a faith that is far deeper than most of us will ever realize exists. In order to remain in this world and to be able to enjoy this world again, there must a complete relinquishment of the pain. There must be a total trust in God that He is watching over your child wherever that child may be. When you place your head upon your pillow in the evening, it will always be with a prayer for your child. Always. But also with an absolute trust in God to answer that prayer.

I read of a heart-wrenching account of a little boy that was missing. He had gone fishing with an older brother and when it was time to go home, the ten year old said that he wanted to stay a while longer. He knew that he could get the fish he wanted if he tried just a little longer. The older brother went on home, not wanting to get into any trouble with his parents. When it was dark, and the ten year old was still missing, a search party was formed. The lake was searched but to no avail. The surrounding wooded area was searched.

Nothing was ever found. Not a clue. Nothing. A missing child. The parents described the absolute nightmare of this ordeal in great detail. Their oldest son lived in anguish, tormented with guilt. Would the sun ever shine for them again?

The mother of this family described in quiet detail how she realized that there still was life all about them. An unthinkable tragedy had occurred. And there were no answers. There were only more questions. In her trusting love, she told how she knew that life must go on or their family would miss the love and joy that they still had. Day by day, she walked, she prayed, and she trusted. One day, as she looked into the burdened eyes of her oldest son, she said she knew it was time to live again. She finally heard the birds chirping. She picked a dandelion from a field. Life goes on. The sun still does shine.

I do not in any way mean to minimize the agony a parent has over a missing child. But, as cold as it may sound, there will come that day when a choice must be made. It will be a very deliberate choice. Do I allow the sun that is shining to warm my cold, broken heart, or do I continue to drown in my sea of sorrow? A choice. Every parent of a missing child will face that choice one day.

Coming to terms with grief is not an easy thing to do. It is similar to being burned by hot coals and telling yourself it doesn't hurt when you know full well that it does hurt. Once the initial pain is gone, new tissue begins to grow over the wound and the flesh is new again. Exactly when this new tissue begins to grow is highly individual. At best, I can say it will happen in time. Time alone does not heal, but time does allow you the precious commodity of getting a new perspective on things.

It is strange how much a parent really can change when a child dies. Once a parent begins that walk into life again, it is with new eyes, a more tender heart, and an entirely new outlook. Problems that once seemed so large do not seem quite so important. Material pleasures do not seem so pleasurable. Somehow, you can now find the time to smell a flower along the path, to marvel over a snowflake, and to look closely at the intricate makings of a bud upon a tree. You are no longer afraid to embrace life. When you feel, it is with an energy and an understanding that you never knew you possessed. Yes. The sun does shine. And it shines ever so brightly.

A husband and wife who have lost a child can have a winding path to tread when working their way back to life. Most likely, the walk will be slow and cautious. But the walk will be made nonetheless. I do believe that this is possibly the most silent, most alone part of child loss for parents. This coming alive again. This coming to know that most assuredly the sun is still shining. This realization that there is life all around you. Life that was meant to be lived. Yes. Even though you no longer have your child, there is still life. This is such a highly personal thing and the timing is so off-balance that I believe this moving towards life must be done somewhat alone, for in the end each of us is responsible for our own choices.

Life is a choice. Your husband cannot make that choice for you. Your wife cannot make that choice for you. That most important decision to go on in life must ultimately be your choice and yours alone. Does that sound harsh? At first, maybe. But after you think about it, the message is quite clear. Up to this point, we really do need the help of others to support, encourage, lift up, prod on, hold, cry with, and listen. After a while, though, we become somewhat more responsible for our actions. This is the part that no one else can do for you. Not even your mate. The sun will never shine for you by someone else's will.

Remember Catherine Marshall? Her husband loved her so, but he could not remove the clouds for her. He could help get her to a certain point, but the actual decision to accept life after loss had to be made by Catherine, and Catherine alone. I would encourage every couple who has lost a child to use extreme patience here. You cannot force anyone back to life. It just will not happen!

I had an experience in my life that explains this quite well. A while back I was quite ill and going through an extremely difficult time of recovery. I was physically weak and my body needed rest. I also needed time to recover. I was told that it would take several months for my body to get strong again. In the midst of these problems, I miscarried a baby very early in pregnancy. This rang the alarm for those closest friends and family around me.

Everything that I did or said was scrutinized, interpreted, and misinterpreted. So, my husband and some well-meaning friends decided that I was depressed and I needed to walk away my depression. (In some people's minds walking is an instant cure-all for everything!) They devised plans to force me to take daily walks. My body was not ready, though. I knew that. I was the only one who really knew how I felt. I was weak and my body sent signals to me that my legs were not ready for walking the steep hills by our home

But on a cold, snowy day my husband and a close friend decided that I absolutely must get outside and walk. Against my wishes I was dressed in a winter coat and boots, and literally dragged outside. The plan was a flop. I was not ready for walking. I was too weak yet. I could not even walk the steps to get off of the porch. I became terribly dizzy and wobbly and was actually put back several days in my recovery due to being forced to do something that I was not ready to do.

What I really needed was time. I knew that this moment was not the right moment for me to walk. Two weeks later I did take my walk. And I enjoyed walking. However, this was a walk that I had to do alone. No amount of forcing would have worked. So it is in child loss. Help is so needed in the early months after a child dies. There is such raw pain and shock to deal with. As time passes, changes occur within each and every parent. Let's call the changes "heart changes." These changes are quiet and subtle. Slowly and surely your eyes are focusing, readjusting to the light you are about to see. What you need now is continuous love and patience as you open up your heart to life again. A push or shove at this time by a well-meaning mate could be so harmful. Remember my walk? I walked when I was ready. I knew myself better than anyone else did, including my own husband.

Coming to the full assurance of knowing that the sun does

still shine, even in your pain, is a choice. It is a choice that you must make alone. Getting to the point of making that choice to see the sun is a slow process. Time is a key factor. Time and patience will produce assurance. Assurance that life has been continuing all along and it is now time for you to enjoy the blessed warmth of the sun.

Every parent who has lost a child longs to get to this point of full assurance of knowing that the sun still does shine. It is a feeling that we desperately long for in our lives. This knowing that things will get better is so vital to reclaiming joy in our lives again. When you already feel so alone in your loss, how do you pull yourself back into life? I believe it is as basic as remembering who God is. Our God is an awesome and powerful God. "And they were all amazed at the mighty power of God" (Luke 9:43). Our God is a God who will never leave our side. "Never will I leave you; never will I forsake you" (Heb. 13:5). Our God wants us to be joyful people. "A joyful heart is good medicine, but a broken spirit dries up the bones" (Prov. 17:22.)

Even though terrible things may come our way, as terrible as child loss, our God is at work in our lives rendering all things for good. "And we know that God causes all things to work together for good to those who love God, to those who are called according to His purpose" (Rom. 8:28). As we are still and reflect on God, we will be sure that God is holy.

We will know that He is Almighty, and He knows what is best in all things. Even in child loss. Most especially in child loss. This is a most difficult precept to really and truly believe during such a period as child loss. We can be assured, though, that in all things God does know what is best. And we know that He can take a terrible situation and bring out some good in it. We must be still and listen to the quiet but powerful voice of God. "Be still and know that I am God" (Ps. 46: 10). We must then let go of our pain and allow God to be God. We must allow the sun that is still shining to shine down on us. It is so warm. His light is so very warm! The sun really does shine! Life is so full of meaning and love. We are surrounded by light of life. And it is just so good. So very good.

Chapter 10

Seeing Beyond Today

Growing up on a chicken farm was a most interesting experience for me. Among those 5,000 chickens cackling and scratching, there were the hens that laid the daily eggs and the boilers and fryers that would eventually go to slaughter. One of my jobs as a young teen was to gather and count the evening eggs, then clean and grade them. I also helped "hook" the chickens that were to be slaughtered each week. By "hook," I mean that I had to use a long-poled tool that resembled a hoe with a curved hook on the end of the pole. This hook would grasp the chicken around the leg, and I would then pull the squawking chicken to me and put it in a crate to be carried off to the slaughter house. I used this procedure on hundreds of chickens each week.

After my first few tries at hooking chickens, it became apparent to me that chickens do not have very good eyesight. At least they do not see the same way as humans do. After all, if they were able to see better, they would not have fallen prey to that hook so easily! I decided to research this thing of the eyesight of a chicken, and I ended up doing a detailed report entitled "The Visual Acuity of a Chicken." I doubt this was a real hot topic to too many people, but it interested me because I had to work with chickens every day. I found out that chickens do not see to the side. They only see straight ahead. In order to have side vision they must turn and cock their entire heads to the side.

That is why I was so good with the hook. Those poor chickens never saw me coming! I wrapped that hook around the leg and snatched up each chicken before it had time to turn its head.

As people, we have the blessing of wonderful eyesight. We have the blessing of eyesight not just in the physical sense, but In a much more meaningful way. We have the ability to "see" each new day as a gift. A blessing, if you will. We can see to the side, as well as straight ahead. In fact, unlike those poor chickens who got snatched by that hook, we can even see a great distance beyond today. We can plan for the future with a hopeful, energetic spirit. When you really stop to think about it, a great portion of our lives is spent seeing beyond today. We hope, we plan, we dream, we strive as we see beyond today. And that is a good way to see life, because in our seeing beyond today we are able to set goals and accomplish often seemingly unattainable tasks, and plan for future peace and happiness.

When a child dies, a parent's eyesight becomes blurred for a period of time. Everything in life looks cloudy and out of focus. After time, though, things come more into focus and we can once again see. Much too often we tend to see like those chickens that we talked about.

We only see what is directly in front of us at the moment. Following child loss, the scene that is before our eyes is one of pain and fear. Emptiness and loneliness find a place right before our eyes, too. As hard as we try, we just cannot seem to turn our heads and look around the corner to see beyond today. That is how much child loss invades our lives. Even our very eyes see differently.

We discussed at length in the previous two chapters the idea of getting to the point where we actually want to go forward in life after the pain of losing a child. This desire to go on is no easy thing to accomplish, and the timetable follows no rules. Equally difficult seems to be the ability to see beyond today, and to do so without the burdens of guilt and fear holding us down. Let me simplify this statement with an illustration. After my 13-year-old sister died, I went through a year of ups, downs, and all-arounds. I really couldn't seem to set my feet on level ground. When I finally did get life back into some sort of proper perspective, things got all mixed up again. I was 16 and I should have been having a carefree, worry-free time of my life. Sixteen is such a great age. There are so many new frontiers to meet.

And there is endless energy. I was no exception to the rule. I was a healthy, energetic, inquisitive 16 year old, but . . . I was different. My family had been crushed by the hand of death. When Carmella, or Mellie as we called her, died, our lives all were changed. Forever changed. When life began taking on meaning again and there was a desire to move on, guilt appeared full force on the scene. There were so many times that I found myself saying to my friends, "No. I can't go with you. I have to stay home." The truth is, I did not have to stay home, but guilt told me that I should stay home. For a long time, I felt that I was somehow being disrespectful, unloving, and selfish if I laughed. When I thought about college, getting married, or having children of my own, I would stop myself. I felt guilty for allowing myself to be happy. Many others may not understand this terrible grip that guilt has, but anyone who has suffered the death of someone close will understand what I am talking about. Parents who have lost a child will know exactly what I am talking about.

Many, many times we do not allow ourselves to see beyond today because we are afraid of losing the memory of our child, or we feel so totally guilty for being happy again. Let me assure every parent that this is not wrong, nor is it bad to think this way for a while. It is quite normal. I would dare to say that every parent that has lost a child goes through this guilt to some degree before that final letting go. We somehow feel that we do not have the right to a happy life any more. After all, a child has died. Your special child has died. And that is not how things are supposed to be. It takes a lot of work to grow beyond this burden of guilt and to be able to see with vision a brighter tomorrow. Hold on. Your dimmed eyes will grow brighter. Each passing day that brings new life will also bring new light.

A young mother talked to me a few months ago as she was experiencing this very guilt that we are talking about. She has a little six-year-old boy. She was ecstatic when she became pregnant again. Only this time she had difficulties in her third month of pregnancy and the baby died.

After almost two years of trying to conceive again, she became pregnant. Everything is going along well this time. The only problem is that this young lady is afraid to be happy. She came to me crying and said she just does not know what to do.

She is so happy with this pregnancy, but feeling so guilty about feeling so happy. After all, she lost a baby.

What this mother is feeling is okay for now. I assured her that these feelings will pass in a short time. She understands that something is off-balance. She should be happy, but she is not. Not completely. She wants to see beyond today, and she can see more than just a glimpse of tomorrow. But she has that gnawing guilt that says, "You are not allowed to be this happy. You lost a child. Remember?" Of course she remembers. She will never forget that painful fact. What she will forget, in time, is that initial searing pain that caused her heart to grieve so deeply. She will continue to grieve, but in a much different way. Her heart will not be heavy like it once was. She will feel energy and life. She will see a bright and happy tomorrow. She will hope and dream. And she will smile. She will smile and her heart will skip a happy, guilt-free beat. And she will look beyond today. She will look towards tomorrow with her eyes opened wide to the beauty all around her.

I really cannot think of anything that invades a heart and robs a person of joy as much as the loss of a child. Many people refuse to even talk about the possibility of such a thing happening. Child loss is that devastating. When financial disasters occur, there are always the possibilities of triumph and great comebacks. When bad health enters the scene, there is always the possibility of a new medication or a different therapy that will cure the illness, or at least offer a reprieve from pain for a while. Such things as divorce, rejection, alcoholism, drug addiction, job loss, prison, or setbacks in life are all tremendous hardships to face. But with each hardship comes the very real, very distinct promise for the possibility of a brighter future. There is hope that circumstances will change and things will get better real soon. There is not that feeling of a final, complete loss with no hope of ever changing the circumstances.

Child loss is different from any other type of loss. When a child dies, there is a finality. There will be no hope of that child getting up and resuming life again. Not in this life. And this is where so much difficulty lies with trying to see beyond today. It is just plain hard to look beyond today in child loss. It is so hard because you know that with every tomorrow there still will be that emptiness. Your child is gone. The place at the table will never seat your child again. You will never hear those words, "Mom. Dad. I love you." You will never see your child through college, a wedding, a first home. You will never share family vacations. That part of your life is gone and it takes an immense amount of effort to get to the point where you can say, "I will be happy again." Seeing beyond today with joy is a tremendous task to accomplish. At times just the mere thought of seeing beyond today without your child seems overpowering.

How does a parent who has endured the crippling pain of losing a child learn to see beyond today? How does a parent pull joy back into the bosom of an empty heart? In talking with many, many parents, as well as feeling the pain of losing a child very intimately, one thing seems to stand out with crisp boldness. Seeing beyond today takes courage. Courage. Raw courage. Along with this courage must come a conscious decision — a choice. A courageous decision must be made to see beyond today. And that decision must be followed by action. Any parent who has lost a child and then goes on to live a joyful tomorrow has fought the most difficult battles of all — grief, isolation, loneliness, discouragement, despair, and guilt, just to name a few. All of these battles took great strength and great courage to overcome. And now, there must be another battle to fight. One that takes the greatest amount of courage. That is the battle of seeing beyond today. Once that decision has been made to see beyond today, half of the battle has already been won. Resolve prompted by courage will carry you through.

It would be easy to write page after page listing all of the organizations that have come about because of child loss. One book that I read lists over 50 pages of such organizations. And, that is noble. We can be so thankful for such resources to offer help. But what about the parent who wants to see beyond today, but is not a courageous, outspoken organizer? What about the silent sufferer who struggles to get to the point of seeing beyond today but knows there will never be an organization named after his child? There will never be a television interview or a book review done about her courageous battle to see beyond today. What about the parent who feels guilt because life is still a struggle two, three, or four years after the death of a child?

I am convinced beyond a shadow of doubt that the majority of parents who have lost a child at any age will have a more quiet, back-seat journey of arriving at the crossroads of seeing beyond today than those who have forged new frontiers along their journey of grief. But this does not mean that they are any less of a person, or that they loved their child any less. Some people just are not comfortable being on the front line. They work better on the sidelines. However, they will reach the goal just the same. I wish that every parent who has lost a child could remember that. Not every parent who has suffered through the grief of losing a child can write a book, give a speech, lead a group, teach a class, or donate a wing of a hospital. But every parent who has lost a child is striving for the same thing. Every parent wants to get beyond the immense pain and reach a point where seeing beyond today is a promising reality.

As mentioned, countless organizations and help groups have come about as a direct result of the therapeutic benefits found in helping others. If a grieving parent can throw all energies into forming a help group or getting a law passed or visiting schools making speeches, somehow a bit of purpose can be found in that child's death. A parent may have the guilt found in going on in life lessened by doing something profoundly beneficial for others. For the majority, though, the grief will remain a silent grief. Because of that fact, we will not spend a lot of time in this particular chapter discussing how to begin a help group as part of your journey to finding a joyful tomorrow. I will mention the benefits of receiving help from such groups. They provide encouragement and support that is most beneficial in getting through those difficult first days of losing a child. As important and as wonderful as these help groups are, not every parent feels comfortable in such a setting. Therefore, we will look at ways that the majority of parents of child loss get to the point of seeing beyond today.

To get to the point of seeing beyond today after losing a child, a parent must learn again to accept life. I know that sounds strange, but it contains so much truth. When a child, your child, dies, so much of life is taken away. I am reminded of this every day when I pick up the newspaper and read the special tributes made on behalf of those who have died. Especially gripping are those tributes written by parents who have lost a child. The message comes through in every line that life is different now. Life is forever changed without your child. There is a joy that is no longer there. It is so terribly difficult to see beyond today and to joy-fully reach into the future without your child.

As I read several of Catherine Marshall's books, I appreci-ated her intense, heartfelt words so much more after I under-stood the pain she endured when her little granddaughter died. When I understood the troublesome journey back to life for Catherine Marshall, her words began to really come alive for me, as well as for millions of other readers. Pain changes people. Pain adds a new dimension to our lives. Pain from losing a child adds a dimension of compassion for others, and a love for life that we did not know was possible. Child loss will tenderize our hearts, if we will allow our hearts to be touched. That is what happened to Catherine Marshall. She finally came full circle back to God and loved Him even more. No. She never, ever under-stood completely why Amy Catherine had to die. No. She never got a full grip on understanding why people must suffer such tragedies. There were many things she did not understand about God and prayer. But this she did know. God was the Lord of her life. God was the giver of all good things, including life. And life was given to be enjoyed.

As her grieving became different several months after the death of Amy Catherine, so did Catherine Marshall's writings. She was able to express her thoughts about God, prayer, love, and life in a way that was even more beautiful, more helpful, more insightful, more meaningful than before. Catherine Marshall was able to see beyond today once again. Her writings reflected this. No doubt, her writing helped move her towards the point of being able to see beyond today, and to look to future days with hope and joy.

As I sat with a group of parents not too long ago, we talked in depth about child loss. There always seemed to be a more quiet hush come about the room when the sacred topic of losing a child came up. That is just how sensitive an issue child loss is. That is why there is still so much silence on the topic. It is in-credibly painful to lose a child. Even years after a child has died, I am finding there still seems to be a corner of a parent's heart that remains darkened. That does not mean that there has not been a full acceptance of the child's death. It just means that there will always be a part of a parent that longs for his child. That is only natural, and I do not think that anyone should try to

176 — Silent Grief

change that. Rather, we should try to understand the intensity of a parent's love for a child better than we do.

As we talked, there were some parents who were active in leading support groups. One mother donates time at a crisis center. One father helps weekly at a soup kitchen. Another father gives of his time doing such things as mowing lawns and.running errands for the elderly. Another young mother is a bereavement counselor at the local school, helping to take care of individual's needs when there is a death in the community. Each person seemed to have found a special niche in life for doing something beyond the normal routine of living.

Interesting. The thing that helped each parent the most to see beyond today seemed to be the act of helping others. Being useful. Finding purpose in living. Living. There is that word again. Living. Life is for the living. Even when your child dies, life is for the living. There is great joy to be found in the dawning of each and every new day. After our heavy hearts have cried a million salty tears, it is time to open our swollen eyes and take in a glimpse of the sun. It is time to form a smile and take in a long deep breath. It is time to look to the expanse of the heavens and realize that God Is still there and He is still in control. It is time to see more than just this day. It is time to see a step beyond. It is time to look towards tomorrow with peace and surety that life does go on.

For a long, long time after my sister Carmella died, my mother struggled with every aspect of life. She just could not seem to find the energy to get through one day, much less entertain the thoughts of seeing beyond today. Six years after the death of my sister, my mother was still struggling every day of her life. She had gone back to work. She made some new friends. She eventually adjusted to me leaving home, going on to college, and getting married. She was managing okay. Not great, but okay. She felt so guilty if she went through a week without crying. My sister's last night alive was tragic, and my mother carried that burden or guilt with her. My sister was living away at a home for terminally ill children and we were only permitted to visit on certain days. Our plans were to visit her all day on Sunday each week. That meant a long day away from home for us, so my mother took me and my little sister to an occasional special night out away from the hospital setting.

This particular Saturday night my mother took us to see a movie. While we were watching the movie, Carmella had her last asthma attack and died alone, without any family by her side, at the age of 13. The hospital tried to call my mother several times, but we could not be reached. My mother carried that horrible, terrible burden of guilt with her for years. The death would have been tragic enough. But to know that the hospital called several times, to know that there would have been time to go to the hospital and be with Carmella before she died, that was a crushing burden to bear.

It was not until January 23, 1971, that I saw an absolute change in my mother. My first daughter, Michelle, was born in Oklahoma City on that morning. My mother, previously afraid to fly, boarded a plane from Philadelphia and came to see her first grandchild. When she held Michelle, the tears rolled down her face as never before. There was life! Beautiful life! There was joy, hope, and promise. There was purpose. For the first time in many lonely years my mother was able to see beyond the many bleak todays. As the tears streamed heavily down her face, I knew that she had found her place in life once again.

My mother never wrote a book. She never spoke to bereaved parents. She never lectured before a large crowd in an auditorium. She never helped legislation to be changed due to her child's death. All of these things would have been good to do. In fact, they would have been great. But, she, like so many other silent grievers, could not move through her grief that openly. The burden of guilt weighed her down. She just seemed to have a more difficult time from the very beginning. Like so very many parents who have lost a child, my mother had a long, difficult, silent journey finding her way back to life. And when she did, it took another life to help her see beyond today. Finally, she found purpose and meaning in living.

Perhaps that is how it will be with you, too. Maybe you have reached the point where you can find some joy in today but you are afraid of your tomorrows. You cannot see any further than the chickens that we talked about in the beginning of this chapter. You need something — someone — some reason — to look beyond today. Be assured that your tomorrows will get brighter. Your vision will come. Your heart will feel life in a new way. Many times in a more meaningful way. And although your grief will never leave, it will be a more subdued grief. Your grief will no longer be your main focal point, but will occupy a quiet corner of your heart instead, allowing you to experience joy today and in the new days to come.

This more gentle type of grieving comes after fighting many battles with questions, fears, deep sorrow, aloneness, and gnawing pain. It may take months, probably years, to reach the point where you honestly feel like you are at peace with today, and you actually anticipate the thought of tomorrow. I believe that trying to rush this process does not help. Time is essential. Time and patience seem to go hand in hand. Because the effects of losing a child, your child, have such lasting consequences, it is only reasonable then to say that it will take time to learn to love life again. To really see beyond today takes a great deal of focused effort and courage.

As I am writing, I am sitting next to my youngest daughter, Alex, as she is sleeping. I recently kissed her forehead and brushed the hair away from her face. She whispered rather groggily, "I love you, Mom." I held her little hand in mine for a long time as I reminded myself once again how very precious life is. And I am reminded every day how fleeting life is. An unexpected illness. A traffic accident. A careless bicycle ride. An accidental fall into the swimming pool. Choking on a piece of candy. These things all sound like remote possibilities, but they happen every day. And when a child dies as a result, lives are forever changed. Lives are forever etched in pain, and it takes a long time to gain enough courage to see beyond today with joy.

My son Joe was mowing and landscaping a yard at a nearby lake last week. He came home for lunch and told me of a life-flight helicopter that landed directly across the lake from him. "There must have been a serious boating accident." The following day, as Joe was reading the newspaper he called me to come into the kitchen. "I feel sick, Mom. The helicopter came to pick up a little boy who drowned at the lake yesterday." On page eight, in small print, there was one tiny paragraph describing the drowning. A three-year-old boy wandered off to the shore of the lake and drowned in six inches of water.

As I have been thinking about this, I realized once again the brevity of life. Life holds so many uncertainties. Children die every day. And lives are dramatically changed because of it.

I do not know the parents of this little boy. But this I do know. They are in pain. They will have a rugged road to travel. There will be a million or more tears shed before they can wake up feeling any joy in their hearts. And it will take many, many painful todays before they reach the point of seeing beyond today, and doing so with a sincere joy.

I would like to mention at this time a thought to those parents who are suffering the loss of a missing child. In different sections of this book the silent grief of missing children has been touched on briefly. I know that justice to this continuous pain cannot be done in the few brief pages of this book, but I feel it is imperative to mention this ongoing grief at this time. In reading the article, "Still Waiting For Jacob," I was reminded in a vivid way once again of the gnawing, relentless pain of this type of loss. Eleven-year-old Jacob was kidnapped at gunpoint by an unidentified man. Today, six years later, Jacob has not been found, but his family continues to search. In this brief article, the idea of coming to terms with the reality of loss is discussed. What interested me the most was how this family finally got to the point of not just living today, but seeing beyond today.

Jacob's family does smile and laugh. This family does celebrate holidays, including a family-time Christmas. This family does have an active, happy household. It is not the same as before. It never possibly could be the same. How could it be? Their Jacob is missing. Six years and he is still missing. It has been a long, slow, difficult journey back to living. And the time of seeing beyond today was a long time in coming. Prayers, a deep spiritual belief, and support of the community have all played a helping hand. Also, the Jacob Wetterling Foundation was formed and is now a $254,00-per-year operation with three full-time employees and a large staff of volunteers. Because of this organization, legislation on sex offenders has been changed. All of these things have been most helpful, most necessary, in helping this family grasp hold of joy today, and to see beyond today.

One sentence about Jacob's family stuck out, though, like a bold banner waving in the sky. It is the sentence that said each parent and each sibling in the family had to make a conscious decision to reclaim some of the joy and laughter that had previously filled the Wetterling home. A decision. A decision to reclaim joy had to be made at some point in time. Once that decision was solid, the joy began filling their lives in slow measures. In order to face this day and the tomorrows of this life, there must be that same conscious decision made to reclaim joy in our lives. Do you remember a couple of chapters back when we discussed choices? Seeing beyond today is a choice, too. For those parents of the many children who have been missing for more than five years this choice may seem impossible today. But with the passage of time and the strength and courage found in prayer, coupled with the caring of others, the choice to see beyond today joyfully must be made.

As cruel and as utterly heartbreaking as it seems, the fact remains that life does continue on despite hardships, devastations, and death. Life is here for the living. It is okay to reclaim some of this joy once again in your life without the weight of guilt holding you down. In fact, it is not just okay, it is necessary to you as parents, and to all of those about you, to reclaim this joy. Yes. You will still grieve your loss. Even if your child is returned to you alive I believe you will always grieve that time of loss which robbed you and your family of any feeling and joy. Child loss changes a heart so permanently. But the silent grief that overtook you in the beginning months will change somewhat. It will not rage within you like it once did. It will be more calm, like the seas after a turbulent storm. You will find that hidden within your heart is the ability to sing a new song.

It is my earnest prayer for each and every parent who has lost a child in this most tragic, unspeakable way to be so surrounded by life all about you that one day you, too, will make that most difficult but necessary choice to go on and to see life beyond today. I pray that you will smile as you face the future knowing that God is by your side. I pray that you will feel His presence all about you, being reassured in small but remarkable ways that God truly does care. You will face that crossroads one day of making that decision. The decision that every parent on earth will be asked to make — whether or not to trust God and choose happiness.

What happens to husbands and wives who are faced with this choice of seeing beyond today? In talking and corresponding with many couples, this, too, is a very individual choice which must be made. Right now I am corresponding with a couple who is in the throes of this very thing. They lost their young adult son to cancer last year. They have journeyed through the many ups and downs of grief, and now they have hit a brick wall. At least that is how they view this problem. The father will not — cannot — see beyond today. He is happy momentarily, but he will not look to the future. That is too painful just yet. He will not schedule time away. He will not plan a vacation. He will not get actively involved in anything extra at church or in the community. Today is all that he wishes to see. The future is too bleak for him without his son.

His wife is terribly frustrated in their marriage because they have locked horns on this issue of not talking about the future. She said that she feels ready to move on. She has cried so many tears that she feels there are no more tears left. She has begun to feel more like her old self with each passing day. She is enjoying life once again, and, as sad as her son's death was, she would like to begin planning for the future again. She would like to plan a vacation, get more involved with people, and talk about more than just yesterday and today. She wants her husband to do these things with her. He views her energy and gaining new enthusiasm as unfair. Their son died. How could they ever be that happy again? His philosophy has become one of living for today. After all, the future is too uncertain of a burden to have to carry.

This very problem of mismatched timing in grief's journey has been cropping up since the very beginning of dealing with losing a child in the husband/wife relationship. No two people meet grief on the same corner at the same time. Not even a husband and a wife. This mother has reached a point in her life where she has said, "I must go on. I want to be happy again. I want to enjoy and appreciate life once more." The father is almost there, but not quite. To push or shove him forward in his grief would be so wrong.

As I talked with this mother, we recalled the patience and time her husband had given her in the first few months after her son died. All she could do was cry. Now it was her time to be patient and understanding. Does that mean that she cannot move on beyond today? Not at all. In fact, her moving on may actually help her husband more than anything else. Many times we must help ourselves before we are able to help anyone else. This is one of those instances. Her husband will eventually pull up alongside of her. He needs a bit more time to shed the guilt and fear that accompany the choice of reclaiming the joy once shared in this family. With loving patience they will see beyond today. Their eyes will have vision and purpose and a sensitivity to all of life. They will experience that rich, full joy that only hearts dripped in pain can feel. The future will hold beauty in their eyes. And they will see beyond today as a couple. And, you will, too. Just give things a bit more time.

Maybe it seems like I am downplaying the importance of being "together" in your marriage relationship on this issue of seeing beyond today in your grief. I am not. Losing your child imposes such demands on your mind, body, and soul that sometimes it is better to back off and allow space, time, and prayers to take over. No one can force this issue of choosing to look beyond today. Child loss is that personal. Grief is that intimate. Pain runs that deep. When you feel like lecturing your mate or lashing — don't. When you feel like forcing the issue — please don't. Remember in a previous chapter when my husband and friend forced me to walk when I was so ill? Forcing did not work. It was too soon. I walked when I was ready. Try to remind yourself of that daily. You cannot push another person's pain away. Not even your mate's pain. You can help by encouraging, listening, praying, talking, and just being there. But you cannot make the final choices for another person.

And this holds true in marriage. Maybe this is more true in marriage, because a husband and wife share such intimacy together that it is expected that you be together in something as personal as your child's death. Dealing with this death is very personal, though. Let go, and let life lead you on to peace and joy. God is in the forefront. He has always been there. Allow Him to lead you. It is that simple. And it is that terribly difficult. It is time to allow God to be God once again. It is time to embrace life again. And you will. In time, you will.

As you travel through this life without your child, you will face many new, often fearsome battles. Most of the battles are long, difficult, and lonely. Remember that your Captain has not deserted you. He is waiting for you, calling you on to a time when you can take a reprieve. Why not choose to see beyond this day and move ahead? Allow your distraught heart to be quieted, and shed the layers of guilt and fear that hold you down. Take a peek around the corner and realize that there is life. Precious life is waiting there for you.

Everyone has a choice. "Choose for yourselves today whom you will serve" (Josh. 24:15). When you feel as though you cannot move beyond today, think of a promise of God. "I will be with you; I will not fail you or forsake you" (Josh. 1:5). When you feel so alone in your grief, know that God is your constant Saviour and guide. "For such is God, our God is forever and ever; He will guide us until death" (Ps. 48:14). When you think your pain is not understood by anyone, remember your Saviour's words. "Then you will call and the Lord will answer; you will cry and He will say, 'Here I am' " (Isa. 58:9). When you think that joy will forever escape you, remember who is the source of all joy. "For great is the Lord, and greatly to be praised. . . . Let the heavens be glad and let the earth rejoice" (Ps. 96:4-11). When you feel like such a failure, remember that you are precious in God's sight. "For God so loved the world that He gave His only begotten Son" (John 3:16). Your child was precious, and now it is time to embrace the fact that you are precious, too. Life was given as a gift to enjoy. It is time. It is finally time to move on and to embrace the precious gift of life. "There is a time to weep, and a time to laugh; A time to mourn, and a time to dance" (Eccles.3:4).

Chapter 11

The Hope of Someday

*The Lord's loving kindnesses indeed never cease,
For His compassions never fail. They are new every
morning; Great is Thy faithfulness. "The Lord is my
portion," says my soul, "Therefore I have hope in
Him"* (Lam. 3:22- 24).

A large part of the fun of planning a trip or saving enough money to purchase something really special is the anticipation that goes along with reaching the ultimate goal. My husband and I experienced just such joy and anticipation when we were striving for several years to reach the goal of purchasing our first home.

Even before my husband and I were married we dreamed of having our own home. We had close friends, the Saunders, who owned a home in the countryside. Every time we visited, we would walk around the paths and down the driveway, viewing the house in the woods, anticipating, hoping, dreaming of that day when we would have our own home. So real was this idea of what our home would be like that I had dream after dream in great detail of "our home."

After John and I were married, reality set in and we understood that our dream was going to take some time and hard work to reach. We found plenty of homes that could easily have fit our description of our dream home, but we lacked one necessary thing. Money. You cannot buy a home without money. During the next

13 years we went through a tremendous amount of pain as we continued to plan and dream of our home. We went from living in a tiny apartment to a rented house to a minister's parsonage. I do not mean to sound ungrateful by any means. We always were most thankful that we had a place to live. However, each place had something missing. A large part of "us" was missing. We never felt that we had nestled into that place we could forever call home.

As the years passed, we continually dreamed of a large, old house in the woods with a long lane leading up to the house on the hill. There would be berry bushes, maple trees (my husband's favorite), and pine trees (my favorite), lots of wildflowers, and privacy. All that we would hear would be the birds singing during the day and the crickets chirping their nighttime songs in the evening. Our home. Someday this would be our home.

The clear reality of life for us was that we lived right smack in the middle of town. We woke up to cars honking horns, fire sirens blowing, ambulances racing past our apartment to the hospital located only one block away. Instead of having the sun shining in our bedroom window, we had the corner streetlight at night light up our room. Rather than breathing fresh night air, and walking hand in hand down a wooded lane, we breathed the heavy odors of Lysol and other disinfectants wafting from the nursing home only a few feet from our kitchen and bedroom windows. There were no berry bushes. There was no wooded land. There were no maple or pine trees. There was pavement. The street was lined with electrical and telephone poles. The only yard was our porch. A far cry from our vision of home!

I will not fill these pages with the ups and downs of our journey to get our home, but I will say that God was directing our lives every step of the way.

In many ways the journey following child loss is similar to so many other struggles in life that we are so often asked to face. Only losing a child is a much more difficult journey and the final goal will not be reached until that great reunion planned in heaven. As I have personally been called on to travel the lonely road following the loss of a child several times now, I am made acutely aware that a final satisfaction, that most endearing peaceful joy, cannot ever be attained while on this earth. That is not to say that a parent who has lost a child can never attain a great measure of

joy while here on this earth. What I do understand quite personally is that there will always be a very intense longing for someday. Someday when God allows that reunion with parent and
child to take place in heaven.

My heart, though overflowing with happiness, still aches.
There will always be a corner of my life that feels incomplete. I
am reminded of this at every family gathering. I am reminded of
this during every holiday. I am reminded of this when I see young
children playing. I am reminded of this when I am told of the
birth of a new baby. That is not to say that I am sad every day; I
am not. But there is a yearning, a longing, a very real anticipation
for that special someday. There is a vacancy that needs to be filled.
And the only way that emptiness will be filled is when that reunion in heaven takes place. Any parent who has lost a child will
identify with this same yearning, this same empty longing.

Every parent who has lost a child knows how special this
hope of someday is. Whether your child died early in a pregnancy or soon after birth, your longing will still be there. Many
times there is a double yearning. Often it is not even known if
your child was a little girl or a little boy. I know that I lost three
girls and one boy. The other children will remain a mystery to
me until I am reunited with them. I am sure that this longing to
see and to know is a strong force kept deep within the heart of
every parent who has lost a child this early.

For parents who have lost a child older than an infant, that
hope of someday carries with it somewhat of a different meaning. I am reminded of a father who lost his four-year-old son in
an automobile accident. He and his wife have adjusted to life
without their son. They have productive, full lives. But . . . there
is that void that absolutely, positively nothing can fill. He said,
with tears running down his face, that when heaven's gates open
he intends to run, not walk, through those gates. This father said
he hopes that everyone will quickly move to the side to avoid a
stampede, for he will be looking among every face in heaven
searching for his son. He plans to run to his son, grab him up into
his arms, and hold him close to his breast for all of eternity. What
a depiction of a father's love for his son. What a reminder that no
matter how many years pass on this earth, the intense longing for
the precious one never, ever goes away. In many ways, I believe
that as a parent grows older the void left by the child becomes

more vivid, and that hopeful anticipation of being reunited again someday becomes more and more real.

As older parents attempt to cope with the loss of an adult child, they will also live with this hope of someday. A dear friend of mine lost her son when he was almost 50 years old. As this mother approaches the end of her earthly life, her tears seem to be a bit less salty. Her moist eyes have a different look. Her entire countenance seems to be quieted. I honestly believe that she has finally made peace with the fact that her son is gone. What is it that made the biggest difference in her life? Hope. That wonderful hope of someday. She is at peace with the thought that she will not just be united with her Lord, but she will also be reunited with her son. That anticipation of her goal of someday reaching heaven sustains her through the difficult days. The hope of someday prods this dear lady on.

In talking with parent after parent who has lost a child, prayer seemed to be a focal point of this idea of the hope of someday. After the angry tears have fallen and a parent no longer feels that betrayal by God, prayer becomes a sustaining force in every parent's life. When I began this book, I asked a large number of parents who had lost a child several questions in order to help me fully understand every type of child loss. One of the questions I asked was, "What helped you the most to get beyond those first tears of loss and to move on in life?". Undoubtedly, 100 percent of the parents questioned said that prayer and the hope of someday helped them the most.

Prayer. A means of communication with God. Talking. Asking. Searching. Pouring out. Accepting. Thanking. Prayer. What a comfort. What a blessing. What a privilege. Have you ever really thought much about prayer and the unlimited power released through prayer? Almost every parent that has had a child die relies heavily on the power of prayer. When a child dies a physical death, we know that the spirit of the child lives on. I know only a small handful of people who claim not to believe this. That spirit goes to be with our Lord. Talking with God, the guardian of that spirit, holds a special comfort. Talking with God through prayer gives a peace that cannot fully be explained in human terms. Being able to talk with God gives us hope in all things — even in the loss of a child. Parents who have lost a child can utilize this power found in prayer to comfort them when nothing else comforts. Parents use this power found in prayer to sustain them when nothing or no one else can. Parents use this power found in prayer to provide that special hope that someday there will be a reunion in heaven where they will one day see their child again. Power. Prayer. Hope. Someday. It all fits together. It is what keeps us together when nothing else helps.

I have had many somber occasions to be in hospitals near gravely ill people. Never once has a person refused the offer to have a prayer together. At gravesides, the final moments before leaving the loved one are spent in prayer. When a parent no longer can touch or hold their child, prayer helps to offer a comfort and quiet strength. When a parent can no longer see the smile on their child's face, prayer calms the soul. When a parent does not know the whereabouts of a missing child and is engrossed day and night in a whirlwind of pain and despair, prayer offers a calming peace that cannot be fully explained in human terms.

Prayer. Asking of God and receiving. Prayer. Trusting completely in God. One mother, after losing her young daughter to leukemia, said that the most difficult time for her was about a year after her daughter's death. She could not seem to enjoy any of the things she once did. Not completely. She never really felt at peace. There was always an inner stirring of her soul. An unrest. One day she decided to make prayer part of her daily existence. She asked for God's help at the beginning of each day. She asked for God's help several times during the day. And she spent time every evening pouring her heart out to God in prayer. She was able to tell God things that nobody else would have ever understood. If we are honest with each other, we all have thoughts that are less than noble at times. Child loss can often bring to surface thoughts that we did not even know we held in the contents of our hearts. Isn't it a blessing that we can go to God in prayer with even the worst of thoughts, knowing that He will still love us? I am so thankful that God has provided a way for me to talk to Him, even when my grief has tainted the color of my thoughts black.

The more we pray to God, the more He becomes an integral part of our being. The more alive He becomes. The more personal His touch is to us. The more we feel His almighty power working within us. If you are closing in on the first chapter of your grief after losing your child, I would strongly urge you to begin the rest of your walk with prayer. Prayer will help to sustain you through the bleakest days. Prayer will steady your faltering walk. Prayer will keep your eyes focused ahead as your journey in life continues on. Prayer will give you balance in your unsteady world. Prayer will give you the comfort of a much-needed friend. Prayer will give you the hope to carry you through this life as you strive to anticipate what lies ahead. Prayer is an essential ingredient to our living. Prayer is the most powerful sustaining force a parent can have when suffering through the personal pain of losing a child, because it fosters hope.

Final Thoughts

As I was driving home the other evening, I was alone in my thoughts. It was a warm night and the stars were shining. The country road I was on was desolate. The farm houses all looked neat and in order. The cows were in the barns and the tractors were silent. I could not wait to reach my home. I had not seen my husband for two days and I missed my time with him and the children. As I drove and heard nothing but the echo of silence, I also heard the resounding presence of God. His presence was everywhere. His presence was in the sky, the stars, the fields. His presence was in the fresh air that I was breathing. He was in the peaceful quiet of the night. I was filled with hope and joy in those moments because I was reminded once again of God and His bountiful love. God is here, all about us. We do not need to feel alone or lonely. We do not need to give in to despair. There is hope all about us. Even in the bitter reality of child loss there is hope.

> *The heavens are telling the glory of God; and their expanse is declaring the work of His hands* (Ps. 19:1).

> *Thy will be done on earth as it is in heaven* (Matt. 6:9).

> *For our citizenship is in heaven, from which also we eagerly wait for a Savior, the Lord Jesus Christ* (Phil. 3:20).

> *And hope does not disappoint, because the love of God has been poured out within our hearts through the Holy Spirit, who was given to us* (Rom. 5:5).

> *And He shall wipe away every tear from their*
> *eyes; and there shall no longer be any death; there*
> *shall no longer be any mourning, or crying, or pain*
> (Rev. 21:4).

As we have traveled this path of such a somber and silent grief together, I hope that your heart has been touched in ways that you never thought possible. It is my most sincere prayer that you have found something written on the pages of this book that has helped.

Every parent who has lost a child has entered a special realm of suffering unknown by anyone else. May you find comfort, as I have, in knowing you are not alone. May you find courage to face the new days ahead. And may you hold fast to the hope that is given to us each new day by a loving Saviour and Friend.

Finally, may the grief that once invaded your heart by such force be a calmed grief. May your now-silent grief color your days with a wiser perception and fuller appreciation of all of life. May your tender heart be warmed, and may your soul abide in love forever.

— Clara Hinton